COMPARATIVE STUDY OF CRIME AND ITS IMPUTABILITY IN ECCLESIASTICAL CRIMINAL LAW AND IN AMERICAN CRIMINAL LAW

THE CATHOLIC UNIVERSITY OF AMERICA
CANON LAW STUDIES
No. 385

Comparative Study of Crime and Its Imputability in Ecclesiastical Criminal Law, and in American Criminal Law

A DISSERTATION
SUBMITTED TO THE FACULTY OF THE SCHOOL OF CANON LAW OF THE CATHOLIC UNIVERSITY OF AMERICA IN PARTIAL FULFILLMENT OF THE REQUIREMENTS FOR THE DEGREE OF DOCTOR OF CANON LAW

BY
REVEREND JOHN J. McGRATH, A.B., LL.B., J.C.L.
PRIEST OF THE DIOCESE OF STEUBENVILLE

THE CATHOLIC UNIVERSITY OF AMERICA PRESS
WASHINGTON, D.C.
1957

NIHIL OBSTAT:

THOMAS OWEN MARTIN, S.T.D., J.C.D., LL.M.
Censor Deputatus

Grandormensii, die 10. oct. 1957

IMPRIMATUR:

✠ JOHN KING MUSSIO, J.C.D.
Episcopus Steubenvicensis

Steubenvicensii, die 10. oct. 1957

Printed by The Abbey Press, St. Meinrad, Indiana

To Mary, the Mother of God, Mirror of Justice and Refuge of Sinners

FOREWORD

The comparison of different systems of law highlights the strong points and the weak features of each system. That which is proper to each system stands out in bold relief. It is, perhaps, only in the making of such contrasts that each is seen in its true perspective. Legislators, while faced with similar problems, do not always solve them in the same way. The nature of the society, the means of enforcement, and a multitude of circumstances of time and place, lead to a growth and development of jurisprudence which is the key to understanding the society from which it springs.

The Ecclesiastical Law of the Roman Catholic Church, and the Civil Law of the United States of America, rule concurrently the lives of modern-day men. Each, within its own sphere, governs in order to guard and protect the common good of the society; each must punish those who transgress the law and inflict injury upon that common good. A comparative study of the criminal law of both systems will enable us to understand each better, and to appreciate the particular merit of each system of criminal law.

To attempt a study of each crime in both systems of law would necessitate a work of far greater length than is permitted here. For this reason the definition of crime, its imputability to its author, and those causes which affect that imputability, are the sole subject matter of this study. The specific crimes and the punishment of crime must be left to another work.

The writer is deeply grateful to His Excellency, the Most Reverend John King Mussio, J.C.D., Bishop of Steubenville, Ohio, for the opportunity to undertake graduate studies in Canon Law, and to the members of the Faculty of the School of Canon Law of The Catholic University of

America for their kind assistance during the course of these studies and in the preparation of this work. It would be something less than justice not to express my indebtedness to the late C. Gerald Brophy, M.A., LL.B., Dean of the School of Law, Duquesne University, whose patient direction and understanding initiated the writer into the study of law.

TABLE OF CONTENTS

CHAPTER I

INTRODUCTION

ARTICLE I. THE CHURCH AND ECCLESIASTICAL CRIMES

The end or purpose of the Church is to lead and help the faithful to attain the sanctification of their lives and thus to procure their supernatural destiny, the Beatific Vision of God.[1] The Church does this through the means commanded or counseled by Christ, and by those means which the Church supplies as they are necessitated by conditions or circumstances existing in the world at a given time.[2]

This care of souls of the faithful is exercised by the Church in two different ways. The individual must render to God an account of his actions, or for the omssion of commanded acts. By the command of Christ this account is rendered here on earth in the internal forum of the sacrament of penance. The Church, acting by delegated power, passes judgment upon sin, the subject matter of confession.[3] With sin, as such, this thesis is not concerned.

The Church is a society, not just a collection of individuals. It is a perfected society with its own proper super-

[1] Bender, *Ius Publicum Ecclesiasticum* (Bussum in Hollandia: Paulus Brand, 1948), p. 34 (hereafter cited as Bender); Ottaviani, *Institutiones Iuris Publici Ecclesiastici* (2 vols., Romae: Typis Polyglottis Vaticanis, Vol. I, 3. ed., 1947; Vol. II, 2. ed., 1936), I, 157-158 (hereafter cited as Ottaviani).

[2] Wernz-Vidal, *Ius Canonicum ad Norman Codicis Exactum* (7 vols. in 8, Romae: Apud Aedes Universitatis Gregorianae, Vol. I, 2. ed., 1952; Vol. II, 3. ed., 1943; Vol. III, 1933; Vol. IV, Pars I, 1934; Vol. IV, Pars II, 1935; Vol. V, 3. ed., 1946; Vol. VI, 2. ed., 1949; Vol. VII, 2. ed., 1951), VII, 32 (hereafter cited as Wernz-Vidal).

[3] Doronzo, *De Poententia* (4 Vols., Vol. II, *De Contritione et Confessione*, Milwaukee: Bruce, 1951), II, 349; Michiels, *De Delictis et Poenis*, Vol. I (Lublin-Polonia: Universitas Catholica, 1934), I, 65 (hereafter cited as Michiels).

natural end, and containing within itself all the means necessary for the attainment of this end.[4] The government of this society, through positive law, is the second way in which the Church exercises its care of souls. This social nature of the Church demands the use of social means. To assure each man of the social means necessary to attain the salvation of his soul and to attain the Beatific Vision, the Church promulgates laws.[5]

Many of these laws are directed to the good of the individual, and are for his guidance and well-being alone. Thus the Church commands all to receive the Eucharist at least during the Paschal season,[6] and forbids clerics to be sureties without permission of their ordinary.[7] The violation of such laws is sinful, as an act of disobedience to lawful authority; but since the good to be obtained is the good of the individual, the violation does not directly affect the public good of the society.

Other laws have the added purpose of protecting the public good of the ecclesiastical society. In forbidding simony[8] the Church has care not only for the souls of the criminals, but also for the disastrous effect such acts have upon the whole society. Likewise, its legislation concerning the seal of confession[9] illustrates the Church's solicitude not only for the rights of the penitent, but also for the public good of the Church. The whole sacrament of penance as instituted by Christ could be seriously undermined if such violation went unpunished.

The ecclesiastical legislator determines which violations of the law are grave, and among these grave violations

[4] Bender, pp. 34-55; Ottaviani, I, 173-193.

[5] "Ecclesiae est, cum debita subiectione erga praecepta divina positiva et etiam praecepta naturalia utpote multa continentia quae etiam in vita supernaturali valent, pro diversitate circumstantiarum statuere, quae a membris suis sint agenda ut finis Ecclesiae attingatur."—Bender, p. 65; cf. Ottaviani, I, 214-224.

[6] Canon 859, § 1.

[7] Canon 137.

[8] Canons 2371, 2392, 727-730.

[9] Canons 2369, 889-890.

he attaches penalties to those which would adversely affect the public good of the Church.[10] The attachment of the penalty to the violation of a law renders the act, or the omission of a commanded act, a crime.

It should be noted that the law discussed in this work has reference only to the criminal jurisprudence of the Latin Church, and not to that of the Oriental Church except in those things which, by their nature, affect it.[11]

The principles of criminal law will be drawn from the universal law of the Latin Church as promulgated in the *Codex Iuris Canonici* by Pope Benedict XV in 1917 with any changes made in the law by the subsequent popes, particular legislation will not be considered. The law of the Code binds all the faithful of the Latin Church no matter where they reside. There is no limitation as to land, nation, color, or language; the authority of the Roman Pontiff is supreme and full in all matters of faith and morals, and in those things which pertain to the discipline and rule of the Church.[12]

Article II. America and Criminal Law

The end or purpose of the State is to assure to each of its members the things that are necessary for a successful and fruitful life here on earth. The State is a perfected

[10] "The legistlator does not consider all transgressions of the moral or ethical order as crimes, but only such which as a matter of public policy are considered to constitute a danger or *damnum* to the social order. It is this disturbance of the external, social order, or the violation of public rights, which penal laws strive to prevent. When prevention has proved fruitless, then penal laws seek to reinstate and restore the social order."—Swoboda, *Ignorance in Relation to the Imputability of Delicts*, The Catholic University of America Canon Law Studies, n. 143 (Washington, D.C.: The Catholic University of America Press, 1941) p. 83 (hereafter cited as Swoboda); cf. also Regatillo, *Institutiones Iuris Canonici* (4. ed., 2 vols., Santander: Sal Terrae, 1951), II, 438 (hereafter cited as Regatillo).

[11] Canon 1.

[12] Canon 218.

society having its own distinct end, temporal beatitude, and the means within itself to attain this end.[13] In the very act by which they asserted their independence from England, the American colonies set forth the purpose of the government they were in the process of establishing. In the Declaration of Independence we read:

> We hold these truths to be self-evident, that all men are created equal, that they are endowed by their Creator with certain unalienable Rights, that among these are Life, Liberty, and the pursuit of Happiness. That to secure these rights, Governments are instituted among Men, deriving their just powers from the consent of the governed.

After years of trial and error, the Constitution of the United States was adopted in 1789. The Preamble to this most important document in the history of government sets forth in clear terms the precise motive or purpose for establishing the United States:

> We, the people of the United States, in order to form a more perfect Union, establish justice, insure domestic tranquillity, provide for the common defense, promote the general welfare, and secure the blessings of liberty to ourselves and our posterity, do ordain and establish this Constitution for the United States of America.

The individual State government is established to foster the same purpose for the citizens of that State. Thus in Allbritton *vs.* Winona, the court explained the role of the State of Mississippi:

> The purpose for which the state exists is to promote the welfare of its citizens—their peace, hap-

[13] "Civitas est communitas perfecta; quod ex hoc (Aristoteles) probat, quia cum omnis communicatio hominum ordinetur ad aliquid necessarium vitae, illa erit perfecta communitas, quae ordinatur ad hoc quod homo habeat sufficienter quidquid est necessarium ad vitam. Talis communicatio est civitas. Est enim de ratione civitatis, quod in ea inveniantur omnia, quae sufficiunt ad vitam humanam, sicut contigit esse."—St. Thomas Aquinas, *In Libros Politicorum Expositio*, (Taurini, Roma: Marietti, 1951), I, 1, 31; cf. Ottaviani, I, 55; Bender, p. 27.

> piness, and prosperty.... The government is the state's agent, created by its Constiution and charged thereby with the duty of accomplishing this purpose....[14]

The individual State must possess the necessary powers to fulfill the purpose for which it has been created. Thus in defining a State, the Supreme Court of the State of Alabama expresses the necessity for the State's possession of the power to accomplish its purpose:

> The State is a body politic or political society organized by common consent for mutual protection and defense, exercising such powers as are necessary for the purpose.[15]

The origin of the power of the civil State is controverted even to this day. Some[16] find the origin of the State's power in a so-called "contract" entered into by its members. Each of the members of the society agrees to give up some of his rights in consideration of others doing the same. The accumulation of these rights constitutes the power of the state. This was the view of Chief Justice John Jay (1745-1829) in Chisholm *vs.* Georgia:

> Every state constitution is a compact made by and between the citizens of a state to govern themselves in a certain manner; and the Constitution of the United State is likewise a compact made by the people of the United States to govern themselves as to general objects in a certain manner.[17]

One of the greatest of common law commentators, Sir William Blackstone, (1723-1780) placed the foundation of society in the wants and fears of the individual citizens.

[14] Allbritton *vs.* City of Winona, 181 Miss. 75, 178 S. 799, (1938); see also Rutledge Co-operative Association *vs.* Baughman, 153 Md. 297, 138 Atl. 29 (1927).

[15] State *vs.* Inman, 239 Ala. 348, 195 S. 448, (1940); see also Thiede *vs.* Town of Scandia Valley, 217 Minn. 218, 14 N.W. 400, (1944).

[16] Hobbes, *Leviathan* (New York: The MacMillan Co., 1947), p. 113; Locke, *Essays on the Law of Nature* (Oxford: At the Clarendon Press, 1954), p. 119; Rousseau, *Du Contrat Social* (Paris: Aubier, 1943), p. 54; Grotius, *De Jure Belli ac Pacis Libri Tres* (2 vols., Oxford): At the Clarendon Press, 1925), II, 9-15.

[17] Chisholm *vs.* Georgia, 2 Dall. (U.S.) 415, 1 L. Ed. 418, (1793).

He rejected the social contract theory for the founding of the society, but held to an association based on want and fear which keeps men living in society.[18]

Others hold to the theory that the State is necessary to man by reason of his social nature. Man is unable to fulfill his needs in the intellectual, material, and social spheres without a society in which to live. Even if the world held no fear for any man, he would still need the company of his fellow man to complete his life. The origin of the power of the State in governing this most necessary society is placed in nature, or more precisely in God, the author of nature.[19]

Chief Justice Sharswood (1810-1883) of the Pennsylvania Supreme Court is in substantial agreement with those who hold to the theory that civil society flows from man's nature, and not from fear. In his comment on the philosophy of Blackstone cited above[20] he wrote:

> Man is by nature a social being. He is made to live in the society of other moral beings. He cannot be contented in a state of solitude. He would rather "dwell in the midst of alarm than reign" in a desert. . . . There must be a controlling power somewhere lodged: and, wherever or whatever it is, that is *Government.*[21]

Whichever theory is held as to the origin of the State's

[18] "The only true and natural foundations of society are the wants and fears of individuals. . . . But though society had not its formal beginning from any convention of individuals, actuated by their wants and their fears; yet it is the sense of their weakness and imperfection that keeps mankind together; that demonstrates the necessity of this union; and that therefore is the solid and natural foundation as well as the cement of civil society."—Blackstone, *Commentaries on the Laws of England, with a Commentary by Chief Justice Sharswood* (4 vols. in 2, Philadelphia: Lippincott, 1898), I, 46 (hereafter cited as Blackstone).

[19] Rommen, *The Natural Law* (St. Louis, Mo.: B. Herder Book Co., 1949), pp. 236-246; Del Vecchio, *Philosophy of Law* translated by Thomas Owen Martin from the 8. ed. (1952), Washington, D.C.: The Catholic University of America Press, 1953), pp. 352-370.

[20] *Supra,* footnote 18.

[21] Blackstone, I, 48-49.

authority, and there are many more, all admit that the civil power has the authority to establish laws, and to attach a penal sanction to those laws, the violation of which seriously affects the common good of the State. The State does have care of the community with the burden of protecting the individual citizen, his rights, and the common good of all. If necessary, and society has always found it so, the State can inflict punishment upon those who violate the common good.

Blackstone had a most clear concept of the common good of the civil community. He saw the common good as not just an accumulation of the individual rights of the citizens, but as the rights of the society as a society:

> ... public wrongs, or crimes and misdemeanors are a breach and violation of the public rights and duties, due to the whole community, considered as a community in its social aggregate capacity.[22]

Not every violation of the law will be of equal importance before the law. Some violations affect only the rights of the individual, others will have such slight effect upon the common good of society that the deterrent of punishment is not warranted. The violation of law which is criminal must be of such importance to the public that punishment is necessary to protect the common good. Private rights are not, *per se,* protected by criminal law.[23]

It follows from the public character of a crime that no individual can, nowadays, bring the criminal to trial; no private right is at stake. If the individual has suffered, his only redress is by way of civil suit, and not through a criminal action at court. The criminal suit must be in-

[22] Blackstone, IV, 4.

[23] "Not every act which is legally wrong is a crime. Private wrongs are redressed by suits between the parties to the wrong. In a criminal prosecution the government itself is a party, and, in theory, the government moves only when the interest of the public is involved. The basis of criminality is therefore the effect of the act complained of upon the public."—May, *Law of Crimes* (4. ed., Boston: Little Brown & Co., 1938), p. 4 (hereafter cited as May).

stituted by the State, which alone has care of civil society. Thus a crime is defined in *American Jurisprudence* as "any act or omission which is forbidden by law, to which punishment is annexed, and which *the state presents in its own name.*"[24]

The legal system of the United States is not an organic whole throughout the land. Each of the forty-eight States has its own statutes on criminal law, which statutes may differ considerably from State to State. The jurisprudence of most of the States is a direct heir of the common law of England.[25] In others[26] the influence of the Napoleonic Code, or the Code of Justinian, can be traced. In general these influences are the historic result of the jurisprudence of the nations which settled particular States. In several of the States the systems of jurisprudence is entirely statutory, with only indirect influence from European systems of jurisprudence.[27]

The Federal Government of the United States since 1789 is a government of delegated powers. In the period between the Declaration of Independence in 1776 and the adoption of the present American Constitution in 1789, only the colonies were sovereign, although united in a Confederation possessing limited authority.[28] Under the Constitution of 1789, the United States is also sovereign, possessing those powers that are specifically delegated to it.

[24] *American Jurisprudence* (58 vols. and Indices, Rochester, N.Y.: Bancroft Whitney Co., 1935-1952), XIV, 1 (cited by Vol. and Section thus: 14 Am. Jur. Crim. Law 1). Italics supplied by the author.

[25] Morris, *Studies in the History of American Law* (New York: Columbia University Press, 1930), p. 11.

[26] McKay, *The Law of Community Property* (2. ed., Indianapolis: The Bobbs-Merrill Co., 1925), p. 4.

[27] In many states the common law is used to fill omissions of the statute law, e.g., in Pennsylvania, West Virginia.

[28] "Each State retains its sovereignty, freedom, and independence, and every power, jurisdiction and right which is not by this Confederation expressly delegated to the United States in Congress assembled."—*Articles of Confederation*, Art. III.

Justice James Iredell (1751-1799) expressed the relationship of the States to the United States in these words:

> Every State in the union, in every instance where its sovereignty has not been delegated to the United States, I consider to be as completely sovereign as the United States are in respect to the powers surrendered.[29]

Residual power is vested in the States or in the people.[30]

There is no common law or foreign system of jurisprudence in the Federal law of the United States. Everything is statutory. The Constitution, the acts of Congress and the decisions of the courts are the fonts from which the criminal jurisprudence of the United States flows. Since the original thirteen colonies shared the common law principles of England, American jurists of the federal courts tended to use the common law system as a model and example. There is a strong indirect influence here.

The jurisdiction of the United States extends to all those, whether citizens or not, who are within the territorial limits of the country, excepting any who are protected by diplomatic immunity or treaty. Citizens of the United States are bound by its laws even while residing outside the territorial limits, at least in some matters.[31]

Any attempt to discuss the criminal law of the United States in an exhaustive manner would demand a detailed examination and comparison of the laws of each of the forty-eight States, and of the Federal Government. Fortunately, textbook writers find a common denominator among these forty-nine legal systems. This common denominator has come into existence through common traditions, common problems, and the unity which exists in a nation.

[29] Chisholm *vs.* Georgia, 2 Dall. (U.S.) 415, 1 L. Ed. 418 (1793).

[30] "The powers not delegated to the United States by the Constitution, nor prohibited by it to the States, are reserved to the States respectively, or to the people."—*Constitution of the United States*, Amendment X.

[31] Blackmer *vs.* U.S., 284 U.S. 421, 76 L. Ed. 375, 52 S.C. 252, (1932); American Banana Co. *vs.* United Fruit Co., 213 U.S. 347, 55 L. Ed. 826, 29 S.C. 511 (1909).

There has been a real effort among the States to come to a uniform law in many fields by adopting uniform codes of law.

No attempt will be made to give footnote reference to all forty-nine jurisdictions. Where notable deviations from the common jurisprudence occur, the deviations will be noted.

Article III. Comparison of the Societies

The Church and State are both juridically perfect societies with their own proper end. The end of the Church is the supernatural beatitude of its members, or the possession of the Beatific Vision; the end of the State is beatitude in this life. Each society has its own proper means to attain its end. The Church has the sacraments, the Mass, and the principles taught by God, and the means that are instituted by the Church itself in view of the occurrence of particular needs at a given moment in history. The State has the systems of control set up by the legislative, the executive, and the judicial branches of the government.

Both the Church and the State are charged with care of the common good, but in different spheres, the one supernatural, the other natural. Each has the obligation to protect the common good by laws, and to inflict punishment for the violation of these laws if it deems it necessary.

The jurisdiction of the Code of Canon Law extends to all Roman Catholics of the Latin Church wherever they reside. The United States has jurisdiction over all within its territorial limits, and, in some instances, over its citizens no matter where they may be.

CHAPTER II

THE DEFINITION OF CRIME

ARTICLE I. THE ECCLESIASTICAL DEFINITION OF CRIME

An ecclesiastical crime is defined as an act or omission which is unjust, is imputable to its author, and which disturbs the social order of the Church.[1] This definition is philosophical and not juridical. It considers crime in its essential aspects, but leaves aside the norms for determining which acts or omissions are to be considered as crimes.

The Code of Canon Law gives the juridical definition of a crime in canon 2195, § 1. A crime is defined as an external and morally imputable violation of a law to which has been added a canonical sanction which is at least indeterminate.[2]

This juridical definition will be studied by way of an analysis of the elements which go to make it up: the objective element, the subjective element, and the juridical element.

SECTION 1. THE OBJECTIVE ELEMENT

The objective element of an ecclesiastical crime is the external transgression of a law which either forbids or commands an act.[3] The act or omission must be not only an act of the intellect consented to by the will, but it must also be an act, or failure to act, involving the corporal faculties of the criminal. It makes no difference whether the violation has actually been witnessed, but the act must

[1] Regatillo, II, 437; Wernz-Vidal, VII, 31.

[2] "Nomine delicti, iure ecclesiastico, intelligitur externa et moraliter imputabilis legis violatio cui addita sit sanctio canonica saltem indeterminata."—Canon 2195, §-1.

[3] Wernz-Vidal, VII, 39; Swoboda, p. 83.

lend itself to possible perception by the senses.[4] It follows that even occult crimes[5] which have been perceived by no one are true crimes.

The formal object of criminal law is to punish those who violate the common good of the society. In every crime there may be injury done to the private rights of another, and there is certainly injury done to the actor by reason of his sin, but these are not the rights which are being protected by criminal law. The disturbance of the public tranquillity, insofar as the members of the society can be, or have been, scandalized or disturbed, is being punished.[6]

Purely internal violations of the law are in no way externally manifested do not violate the social order. Such thoughts may be sinful and subject to penalty when presented for the sacrament of penance, but they can never be crimes subject to punishment by the Church in the external forum.[7]

The external violation must be a violation of law. Which law? *Per se* and directly a violation of the ecclesiastical law. The Church is competent to punish those crimes which offend the common good of the ecclesiastical society. Often the Church will make a law to be its own law though it already binds the Church's subjects by reason of the divine law, whether natural or positive.[8] Such crimes con-

[4] Michiels, I, 66; Regatillo, II, 438.

[5] Canon 2197, 4°.

[6] Michiels, I, 70.

[7] "De peccatis quis tenetur reddere rationem coram Deo, vel eius ministro, qui loco Dei in foro interno iudicat et punit. De delictis quis tenetur respondere in foro externo, coram societate, quia delinquens ordinem socialem exturbavit. Cogitationes, utpote quae latent ordinem externum, natura sua a iure poenali exulant omnio (cogitationis poenam nemo patitur)."—Roberti, *De Delictis et Poenis* (2 vols.; vol. I, 1930; vol. II, 1938, Romae: Apud Aedes Facultatis Iuridicae Ad S. Apollinaris), I, 54 (hereafter cited as Roberti).

[8] Coronata, *Institutiones Iuris Canonici* (5 vols., Taurini-Romae: Marietti, Vol. I, 4. ed., 1949; Vol. II, 4. ed., 1951; Vol. III, 3. ed., 1948; Vol. IV, 3. ed., 1948; Vol. V, 3. ed., 1951), IV, 5 (hereafter cited as Coronata); Regatillo, II, 438.

travene God's law, and will be punished by Him; they are the subject matter of the Church's jurisdiction in the sacrament of penance. By reason of enactment into ecclesiastical law, these same acts constitute a violation of Church law, and are subject to punishment by the Church in the external forum.[9]

Canon 2220, § 1, states that anyone having the power to pass laws or impose precepts has the power to add a penalty for the violation of the law or of the precept. Among those possessing the power to enact criminal laws must be included: The Roman Pontiff, Councils, the Sacred Congregations, local ordinaries (exclusive of vicars general lacking a special mandate), cathedral chapters, and vicars capitular, and the chapters and major superiors of exempt clerical religious communities according to the norms of their constitutions.[10]

SECTION 2. THE SUBJECTIVE ELEMENT

In order that a violation of law constitute an ecclesiastical crime, the violation must be imputable to the delinquent. Imputability is that property of an action in virtue of which it can be attributed to some person as its proper author.[11]

If the delinquent is free and enjoys the use of reason, the criminal act is to be acknowledged as morally imputable to its author. Moral imputability postulates that the act flow from a human agent who has both the use of reason and a will which is free in its choice. Such acts take on the added note of being good or evil depending upon the purpose for which they are done, the means used, and the circumstances surrounding them. It is postulated for all crimes that the violation of the law be morally imputable to its author, the delinquent.[12]

[9] Michiels, I, 63.
[10] Coronata, IV, 86.
[11] Regatillo, II, 438; Wernz-Vidal, VII, 43; Swoboda, p. 85.
[12] Michiels, I, 82-86; Coronata, IV, 7.

The knowledge postulated for the imputing of an act as criminal to its author includes the knowledge that what is being done is unlawful. The act must proceed from the agent's free will with advertence in the intellect to its malice. The delinquent must be guilty of a grave sin before God and his own conscience. Man is subject to the moral law because of his moral nature in that he has the use of his intellect and a free will; man is subject to penal law because of his social nature in that he is a member of society. If an agent is impeded from performing a moral act, he is likewise impeded from performing a criminal act.[13]

SECTION 3. THE JURIDICAL ELEMENT

A penal law is one which commands or forbids an act under threat of penalty for the transgressor.[14] To constitute a crime in ecclesiastical law, there is postulated the transgression of a law to the violation of which has been attached a penalty of at least an indeterminate character.[15] The addition of the threatened penalty in the law provides the juridical element for the definition of a crime.

There are many laws to which no penalty has been attached for their violation, e.g., canon 859, § 1, which commands the faithful to receive Communion during the Easter season. The violations of such laws are sinful if there is moral imputability, but they do not constitute crimes. For an act to constitute a crime the legislator must have made the judgment that the violation of his law will so seriously affect the social order that a penalty is to be imposed for its transgression. Failure to legislate the penalty results in failure to legislate a criminal law.[16]

[13] Michiels, I, 98; Swoboda, p. 88.

[14] Regatillo, II, 440; Wernz-Vidal, VII, 44.

[15] Canon 2195, § 1; "The penal sanction is sometimes specifically determined; sometimes, however, it consists merely in a general threat of punishment."—Swoboda, p. 84.

[16] Regatillo, II, 440.

The penalty to be imposed in a criminal law need not be specified in detail in the law. The legislator may leave the determination of the penalty to the prudent decision of the judge or the superior. Such a penalty is called indeterminate in the law.[17] It is sufficient if the legislator threatens some penalty if his law is violated. If grave scandal was given, or if the transgression was of a particularly grave nature, a legitimate superior can invoke punishment for the transgression of any law, even if no penal sanction is written into the law. This extraordinary power to punish does not require the superior to threaten the delinquent beforehand.[18] This same power is not, however, given to a judge.[19] Thus the law always threatens a penalty in some way, i.e., by threat of a specific penalty, by threat of some indeterminate penalty, or by the threat contained in canon 2222, § 1, in cases of scandal or particularly grave transgressions.

Article II. The American Definition of Crime

Since the common law of England is the legal ancestor of the law of most of the States, and even, by way of example, of the Federal Government, the definition of a crime at common law is a good starting point for arriving at a definition which will be accurate for most of the modern systems. Blackstone gave the following definition of a crime:

> A crime, or misdemeanor, is an act committed, or omitted, in violation of a public law, either forbidding or commanding it.[20]

This definition specifies the physical element of a crime, but leaves out the mental and legal elements.

The New York Penal Law spells out more specifically the legal element, but is deficient in specifying the mental element, or the criminal intent. The statute reads:

[17] Canon 2217, § 1: "... indeterminata, si prudenti arbitrio iudicis vel Superioris relicta sit sive praeceptivis sive facultativis verbis."

[18] Canon 2222, § 1. [19] Coronata, IV, 90. [20] Blackstone, IV, 5.

> A crime is an act or omission forbidden by law, and punishable upon conviction by:
>
> 1. Death; or
> 2. Imprisonment; or
> 3. Fine; or
> 4. Removal from office; or
> 5. Disqualification to hold any office of trust, honor profit under the state; or
> 6. Other penal discipline.[21]

The definitions found in *Corpus Juris Secundum,*[22] and in *American Jurisprudence*[23] are likewise deficient in spelling out the mental element of a crime. The definition of John Wilder May suffers from this same defect.[24]

A more complete definition, and the one which is adopted here, is offered by William L. Burdick in these words:

> A crime is the voluntary commission, or omission, by a person having criminal capacity, of any act, in violation of a public law either prohibiting or commanding it, and which is punishable by the offended government by a judicial proceeding in its own name.[25]

[21] *The Consolidated Laws of New York Annotated* (St. Paul, Minn.: West Publishing Co., 1955), Penal Law, sec. 2 (hereafter cited as *New York Penal Law*).

[22] "A crime is a wrong directly or indirectly affecting the public, to which the state has annexed certain punishments and penalties, and which it prosecutes in its own name in what is called a criminal proceeding."—*Corpus Juris Secundum* (95 vols., Brooklyn, N.Y.: The American Law Book Co. (1936-1957), XX, 1 (hereafter cited by Volume and section thus: 20 C.J.S. 1).

[23] "Any act or omission which is forbidden by law, to which a punishment is annexed, and which the state prosecutes in its own name."—1 Am. Jur. Crim. Law 2.

[24] "Crime is a violation or neglect of legal duty, of so much public importance that the law, either common or statute, provides punishment for it."—May, p. 1.

[25] Burdick, *The Law of Crimes* (3 vols., Albany: Matthew Bender & Co., 1946), I, 68 (hereafter cited as Burdick); Commonwealth *vs.* Smith 266 Ua. 511, 109 Atl. 786, (1920); U.S. *vs.* Eaton, 144 U.S. 677, 12 Sup. Ct. 764, 36 L. Ed. 591 (1892).

This definition states explicitly the three essential elements of a crime in American civil law:

a. The mental element: "the voluntary commission, or omission, by a person having criminal capacity";
b. The physical element: "of an act, in violation of a public law either prohibiting or commanding it";
c. The legal element: "and which is punishable by the offended government by a judicial proceeding in its own name."

SECTION 1. THE PHYSICAL ELEMENT

"The physical element is the prohibited thing done or the commanded thing left undone, or what is called 'the act.' "[26] Two qualities must be present in the act: the act must have a physical causal relationship to the violation of the law, and it must be an act that is forbidden, or commanded, by the law.

For an act to be criminal it must be so causally connected with the effect as to have a positive influence upon the effect. Mere dispositive causality, or setting the stage for the causative act, will not suffice for a criminal act.[27] Thus, in the case of the People *vs.* Rockwell,[28] the defendant struck the deceased to the ground, who was thus in a position to be trampled to death by a horse. The court rightly held that there was no crime of manslaughter, because the defendant was not guilty of any act which was the cause of death.

The act must have taken place. Mere intention to act without fulfilling the intention is not a crime, but the mere intention should not be confused with attempts wherein the crime, while begun in some external manner, was not completed. The criminal act is required in its complete-

[26] Burdick, I, 106.

[27] "An act to be criminal must be so connected with the intended crimes that it is either wholly or in part cause or tends to cause it." —Burdick I, 111.

[28] People *vs.* Rockwell, 39 Mich. 503 (1878).

ness as an act.[29] The Roman Law expressed this same concept in these words:

> There must be an act and an intent. A mere intention to steal is not theft.[30]

This principle is found in all of the American jurisdictions.[31]

The necessity of a complete, external performance of the criminal act was apparent to the common law, which recognized that the State had no jurisdiction in the internal forum of conscience. Indeed, the state is without the means to search the heart of its subject, and hence to pass judgment. Blackstone had a very clear and precise statement to this effect:

> Indeed, to make a complete crime cognizable by human laws, there must be both a will and an act. For though, *in fore (sic) conscientiae* a fixed design or will to do an unlawful act is almost as heinous as the comission of it, yet as no temporal tribunal can search the heart, or fathom the intentions of the mind, otherwise than as they are demonstrated by outward actions, it therefore cannot punish for what it cannot know.[32]

The criminal act is often called the *corpus delicti,* i.e., the body of the crime. In trial of a case, proof of the *corpus delicti* is the first order of business. Unless it can be proved that the forbidden act was perpetrated the com-

[29] "A criminal act being required in every crime, it follows that, regardless of how positively one may intend to act, nevertheless, if there be no act there is no crime."—Burdick, I, 107.

[30] *Corpus Iuris Civilis,* Vol. I, *Institutiones*—recognovit P. Krueger; *Digesta*—recognovit T. Mommsen, retractavit P. Krueger; opus Schoellii morte interceptum absolvit G. Kroll (Berolini, 1928-1929). See in particular D. (47.2), I D. (47.2) 52.19).

[31] Chandler *vs.* State, 141 Ind. 106; 39 N.E. 144 (1894); State *vs.* Rider, 90 Mo. 54, 1 S.W. 825 (1886); Ex parte Smith, 135 Mo. 223, 36 S.W. 628 (1898).

[32] Blackstone, IV, 21; see also U.S. Constitution, Art. III, sec. 3, on the overt act; U.S. *vs.* Frick, 259 Fed. 673 (1919).

mon good has not been injured, and no further business is before the criminal court.[33]

This has led to the mistake of referring to the dead corpse in murder cases as the *corpus delicti.* It is difficult to prove that a murder has taken place without a corpse, but the corpse is not the criminal act. The *corpus delicti* is the act which deprived the deceased of his life.[34]

Finally, the criminal act must be an action which is prohibited by the law. The individual may intend to violate the law, but if he performs an act which the law does not forbid, there is no criminal act. Again, the State cannot take cognizance of a man's conscience. This last point is demonstrated clearly in the case of Respublica vs. Malin.[35] The defendant intended to join the army of the English in the revolution which freed the colonies from the servitude of Britain. By mistake he joined the army of the revolutionary forces led by George Washington. He had his armies mixed up, and though he intended to be a traitor to the colonies, and although he did an act which he thought would be treasonable, he never committed a crime. The Supreme Court deplored the state of mind of the defendant, but found him guiltless of any crime. He had not performed an act forbidden by the law.

The criminal act must be causative, actually placed and not merely intended, and in violation of the law.

SECTION 2. THE MENTAL ELEMENT

Coupled with the criminal act, there must be a criminal intent.[36] The amount of confusion surrounding the notion

[33] "The *corpus delicti* is made up of two things: first, certain facts forming its basis; and secondly, the existence of criminal agency as the cause of them."—Pitts *vs.* State, 43 Miss. 472 (1870).

[34] Stringfellow *vs.* State, 26 Miss. 157 (1853), wherein the court refused to sustain a guilty verdict based upon a confession in a case where the *corpus delicti* had not been proved independently.

[35] Respublica *vs.* Malin, 1 Dall. (U.S.) 33, 1 L. Ed. 25 (1778).

[36] "It has been the general attitude of the authorities in the criminal law to insist that there can be no crime without the co-

of criminal intent in the various jurisdictions is great, and the problem will be dealt with at greater length in the following chapter.

The voluntariness of the act must be kept separate from the intention to inflict injury or to violate the law. The criminal act must be voluntary, that is, it must flow from the will of the delinquent. Justice Holmes (1841-1935) expressed the necessity for the voluntary in these words:

> An act is a muscular contraction and something more. A spasm is not an act. The contraction of the muscles must be willed.[37]

This voluntariness is predicated upon man's possession of a free will. Unless a man is free to act or not to act, there is no basis for imputing the act to him as criminal.

Criminal intent has reference to this free will in action.[38] Does the concept of criminal intent include an evil purpose, a hardness of heart, a knowledge that the action is evil and a violation of the law? Does the criminal have to know that his action is criminal? In short, is a criminal minds, *mens rea,* a requirement for the commission of a crime?

The doctrine of *mens rea* is to be found in much of the jurisprudence of the Anglo-American law. In more recent times the doctrine has been watered down until there is little left but the words. There is not even agreement on what, if anything, the doctrine means in American criminal jurisprudence.[39]

The greatest inroads upon the doctrine of *mens rea* have been made in the field of statutory crimes, and of acts

existence of (1) an act, or a failure to act, in opposition to a rule of law, and (2) a certain mental element which is known as criminal intent."—May, p.3.

[37] Holmes, *The Common Law* (Boston: Little Brown & Co., 1881) p. 54.

[38] "In criminal law, intent means a state of mind which willingly consents to the act that is done, or free will, choice, or volition in the doing of an act."—Burdick, I, 126.

[39] "There is no general agreement as to what *mens rea* means." —Burdick, I, 162.

prohibited not because they are evil in themselves, but for the sake of protecting public health, morals or safety. Absolute liability, which ignores the state of mind of the agent, is attached to the violation of the statutes. Our courts have sustained these statutes.[40]

The legal mixims, *error iuris nocet,* and *ignorantia legis neminem excusat* have come into full sway in the Anglo-American jurisdictions. There is a strong tendency for all jurisdictions to invoke the principle of absolute liability. If the act is done, then the agent has committed the crime. Ignorance of the law will not excuse. The law tends not to interest itself in whether the mind of the criminal was guilty or innocent, but stops simply with the question of whether he has performed the criminal act. The concept of *mens rea* has disappeared in the major part of our law.[41]

Much of our criminal law has been codified by the various legislatures. These statutes will replace the common law elements of each crime if the statute is in conflict therewith. In general the statutes have retained the concept of *mens rea* in the common law crimes, but the new statutory crimes must be studied carefully to determine whether *mens rea* is part of the crime or not.[42]

SECTION 3. THE LEGAL ELEMENT

Modern legal systems, and those of the United States

[40] Impure foods: Lansing *vs.* State, 73 Neb. 124, 102 N.W. 254 1905); Milk: Com. *vs.* Wheeler, 205 Mass. 384, 91 N.W. 415 (1910); Liquor to minors: State *vs.* Schull, 66 S. Dak. 102, 279 N.W. 241 (1931); Drugs: U.S. *vs.* Balint, 258 U.S. 250, 66 L. Ed. 604, 42 S.C. 301 (1922); Oleomargarine: Com. *vs.* Weiss, 139 Pa. 247, 21 Atl. 10 (1891).

[41] "The rule has developed that in all regulatory penal law mistake of fact is no defense. Thus, the ancient and sancrosanct maxim of common law, *actus non facit reum nisi mens sit rea,* has been abrogated in a major part of our penal laws today."—Mueller, "Mens Rea," *West Virginia Law Review* (Morgantown, W. Va.: University of West Virginia Press, 1894-1957), LVIII (1955), 34.

[42] Burdick, I, 141.

specifically, do not give the judge discretion to punish the violation of laws which have no legal penalty threatened in the law. The common law did give the judge such discretionary power, but such power has been taken from the American judge.[43] The law must, furthermore, specify the penalty to be inflicted. To label a violation of the law as a crime will not suffice. There must be a definite threat of a penalty.[44]

ARTICLE III. COMPARISON OF THE DEFINITIONS

The definition of a crime in ecclesiastical law and the definition as found in American law have striking similarities, but at least one important difference. Agreement is found in the objective or physical element, and in the legal element; the disagreement is found in the mental or subjective element.

The ecclesiastical crime must be an external violation of the law; the crime in American law must be an act in violation of a public law either prohibiting or commanding it. In both cases the violation must relate to an existing law, and the transgression of that law must be external. Mere internal violations of the law do not offend the common good of either society, and hence are not cognizable by the criminal law.

To each ecclesiastical law there must be added a penal sanction, at least indeterminate, if the violation is to constitute a crime. Superiors may punish transgression of

[43] "The English common law judge had an inherent and discretionary power to punish violations of law in the absence of a statute regulating the punishment, but the authority of our judges is created by constitutional and statutory provisions, and punishments for crime in our country are specified by the same means. If a statute creates a public offense but makes no provision for its punishment, no penalty can be inflicted."—Burdick, I, 69-70.

[44] "Saying that it is prohibited, calling it a crime, or stigmatizing it as unlawful is not enough; a punishment must be prescribed." —Orville Snyder, *Criminal Justice* (New York: Prentice Hall, Inc., 1953), p. 9 (hereafter cited as Synder).

non-penal laws if grave scandals or a special gravity is connected with the violation. American criminal law demands that the offended government state the penalty explicitly in the law. Both governments, ecclesiastical and civil, bring the action in their own name as the guardian of the common good of the society.

Both the ecclesiastical and the American criminal jurisprudence demand that the act be done by one having the use of his intellect and a free will. Any interference with the operation of either of these faculties in the performance of the act will take away it full voluntariness, and thus destroy or at least diminish imputability.

The ecclesiastical criminal law demands further that the criminal be guilty in his own conscience and before God for the transgression. Ignorance of fact or of law may excuse or diminish the imputablity of the crime.

The concept of a guilty mind, or a *mens rea,* is no longer a strict requirement of American criminal jurisprudence. *Mens rea* was required at common law, but inroads have been made upon this principle in modern times. In statutory crimes, and especially with reference to statutes aimed at protecting the common good in the cases of foods, drugs, morals, and public safety, the legislatures have adopted the principle of absolute liability. In these crimes, which are a major portion of criminal jurisprudence, the state of mind of the criminal is not considered.

CHAPTER III

THE IMPUTABILITY OF CRIMES

ARTICLE I. IMPUTABILITY OF ECCLESIASTICAL CRIMES

SECTION 1. ECCLESIASTICAL LAW AND THE MORAL ORDER

The moral order is composed of all those acts which have the property of rightness or wrongness, so that they can be imputed to the author of the act. There is no human act that is not part of the moral order, for every human act, flowing from the intellect and free will of men, is either in accord or at variance with right reason.[1]

In spite of the wide diversity of possible human acts, there is a real unity in the moral order. All men have a common final end in life—eternal beatitude. The actions of a man's life take him either toward, or away from, this ultimate goal. The moral order, materially made up of the sum total of man's actions, dictates whether these acts are good or bad in their end, and in the means used to attain that end.[2]

Man does not attain his eternal destiny alone, but rather by living in society. The State and Church alike have the right to lay down norms of conduct for the individual. The violation of these norms or laws is a violation of the moral order. If the law has a penal sanction attached to it, the legislator has deemed the transgression to be a serious violation of the moral order.

It follows that the moral order, and the juridical—including the criminal—order are not separate and distinct. Since the juridical-criminal order is but one part of the

[1] "Ordo moralis est ordo illorum elementorum, quae sunt praedita moralitate. Haec sunt actus humani."—Bender, *Philosophia Iuris* (Romae: Officium Libri Catholici, 2 ed., 1955), p. 224.

[2] "Finis ultimus efficit, ut omnes actus humani uniantur et sic aliquod 'unum' sint per hoc quod omnes actus ad unum bonum ordinantur tamquam media."—*loc. cit.*

moral order,[3] the principles used in the moral order will apply also in the juridical criminal order. The moral order requires that an act be morally imputable to the author of the act if he is to be held responsible for it. This same principle must apply in the juridical-criminal order.[4]

The juridical-criminal order will have, however, some principles of its own, which flow from the nature of criminal law. The moral order can proceed from the evil internal act to any outward manifestation of the evil mind; criminal jurisprudence is without the ability to start with the internal act, for it must start with the external act and work back to the criminal mind.[5] With this one exception kept in mind, the nature of imputability can be drawn from moral principles and applied to criminal law. The resulting principles will make up the jurisprudence of criminal imputability in ecclesiastical law.[6]

SECTION 2. IMPUTABILITY IN GENERAL

Imputability is that property of an action in virtue of which it can be attributed to some person as its proper

[3] "...ordo moralis et ordo iuridicus non sunt duo ordines omnio distincti et separati, sed ordo moralis complectitur ordinem iuridicum sicut totum complecitur suam partem."—*Op. cit.*, p. 223; Michiels, I, 98.

[4] Michiels, I, 99; "Now, since according to the fundamental principles of human reason the moral order cannot be injured except by acts morally imputable to the agent, so also the juridic-social order, which is a constitutive part of the moral order, cannot be injured except by external acts morally imputable to the agent." —McCoy, *Force and Fear in Relation to Delictual Imputability and Penal Responsibility*, The Catholic University of America Canon Law Studies, n. 200 (Washington, D.C.: The Catholic University of America Press, 1944), p. 56 (hereafter cited as McCoy).

[5] "...*in foro externo*, e contra, praeprimis attenditur factum externum illudque semel verificatum regulariter *praesumitur* culpabiliter positum..."—Michiels, I, 100. (Italics supplied by writer.)

[6] The very definition of an ecclesiastical crime as given in canon 2195, § 1, directs our attention to moral imputability when it uses the words *moraliter imputabilis*.

author.[7] Not only the act itself, but all of its properties and effects are attributable to the author of the act. The practical judgment that an individual was the author of a particular act is called imputation.[8]

It is fundamental to imputability that there be a physical, causal connection between the agent and the action so that the agent becomes the true efficient cause. Such physical causality can be predicated even of animals and of persons bereft of reason. Thus the blasphemy of the insane is physically imputable to the speaker, and can rightly speak of dogs as having chewed up rugs.[9]

The moral order, however, is concerned only with human acts, such as flow from the intellect and free will of man. Bare physical efficient causality is not enough; moral imputability concerns itself only with those actions over which man is the master, or, in the words of St. Thomas Aquinas, over which he has the *"dominium sui actus."*

Moral imputability always has reference to the rightness or wrongness of the act. When the action is in conformity with the moral order, or with the norms of morality, it is a good or moral act; it is evil or immoral if it deviates from the norms of morality. It follows that there must be some advertence of the intellect and a consent of the will to the goodness or evilness of the action in the performing of the act. If the agent performs an objectively evil act with no advertence to its malice, and with no intention to do evil, the evil cannot be imputed to him.[10]

Once an act has been imputed to a man as good or evil, the question of responsibility can arise. Responsibility is the relation of the agent to another to whom he must render an accounting for his action.[11] Thus the servant is responsible to his master, and the agent is responsible to the principal, since each of these must render an acount

[7] Michiels, I, 83; Regatillo, II, 438; Wernz-Vidal, VII, 43.
[8] Regatillo, II, 439.
[9] Regatillo, II, 438; Wernz-Vidal, VII, 43; Michiels, I, 83.
[10] Michiels, I, 85; Coronata, IV, 7.
[11] Regatillo, II, 439; Roberti, I, 86; Coronata, IV, 7.

to his superior. It is for this reason that we can impute actions to God, e.g., creation, redemption, but God is not accountable or responsible to anyone.[12]

Responsibility can be of a purely moral character, e.g., the responsibility one has to render to God an account of his actions. When this account is rendered to God in the sacrament of penance, which He established, there is involved a juridical-moral responsibility. The subject matter of this type of responsibility is sin. Here the sinner renders to God's representative an accounting for the transgressions of the law of God.

Inasmuch as man is meant to live in society, he must answer to society for his actions; he is responsible to society. This responsibility is called a juridical-social responsibility, because it affects the juridical structure of the society. When the act is contrary to the criminal law of the society, the accounting is referred to as juridical-criminal responsibility.[13]

SECTION 3. THE BASIS OF JURIDICAL-CRIMINAL IMPUTABILITY

What are the fonts of juridical-criminal imputability? In consequence of the principles of morality one can find two fundamentals upon which to base the imputability of criminal actions: malice and criminal negligence. These fundamentals are delineated in canon 2199, which states that the imputability of crime arises from the malice of the delinquent, or from his negligence either in being ignorant of the law he violates or in omitting the diligence he owes.[14]

Malice

Dolus, or malice, is the deliberate will to violate the

[12] Roberti, I, 87; Coronata, IV, 7; Regatillo, II, 439.
[13] Michiels, I, 86; Wernz-Vidal, VII, 44; Regatillo, II, 439.
[14] Canon 2199—"Imputabilitas delicti pendet ex dolo delinquentis vel ex ejusdem culpa in ignorantia legis violatae aut in omissione debitae diligentiae. . . ."

law.[15] In the word *deliberate* is expressed the need for the operation of the intellect; in the word *will* is found the necessity for the command of the will.

The criminal must know before he acts that his prospective act is contrary to the law or to a legal obligation, and he must have sufficient deliberation on this matter to have actual advertence to the illegal character of the external act he is about to perform.[16] It is not necessary for the agent to know that a penalty has been added to the law's violation,[17] but ignorance of the penalty will diminish culpability.[18]

The will of the delinquent must be free in this concrete case. Actions which are so spontaneous or reflex that the will has had no part in them cannot be adjudged malicious acts.[19] Further, there must be the positive will to perform this determined act which the intellect already knows to be contrary to the law.[20] In this latter consideration there should be no confusion between the motive and the intention.

The reason why a person acts may appear to him as a good thing, although in fact it be contrary to law. He may even wish that the act were not forbidden by the law. It is sufficient for *dolus*, or malice, that the act is known to be in violation of the law, and is done willingly, no matter what the motive of the agent may be.[21] Thefts, for

[15] Canon 2200, § 1—"Dolus heic est deliberata voluntas violandi legem. . . ."

[16] ". . . tum cognitio legis contra quam ponitur actus seu scientia obligationis legalis . . . tum deliberatio seu advertentia actualis ad characterem antijuridicum actus externi positi . . ."—Michiels, I, 102-103. Cf. also Wernz-Vidal, VII ,62; Regatillo, II, 447.

[17] Michiels, I, 102.

[18] Canon 2202, §2—"Ignorantia solius poenae imputabilitatem delicti non tollit, sed aliquantum minuit."

[19] ". . . libertas agendi in casu concreto de quo agitur . . ."—Michiels, I, 102.

[20] ". . . voluntas actualis positiva ponendi actum determinatum, qui cognoscitur legi contrarius . . ."—Michielis, I, 103.

[21] ". . . quamvis non intendat legis violationem qua talem, sed aliud intendat, mediante violatione."—Regatillo, II, 447; Michiels, I, 103.

whatever motive, are still thefts, and thus remain violations of the law.

Since the definition of malice postulates the use of the intellect and free will of the criminal, anything which would diminish or take away the use of either of these faculties would also take away or diminish the malice and the imputability of the crime.[22] This subject will be treated at length in a subsequent chapter.

The performing of an external violation of the law raises the presumption in the external forum of the presence of malice, unless the contrary is proved.[23] The rules governing such presumptions of law are found in canons 1825-1828.

Criminal Negligence

The role of the legislator in any society is to safeguard the juridical-social order, or the common good. When the legislator obliges his subjects to avoid malicious violations of the penal law, he is directly protecting the common good from injury. The legislator can, and indeed has a duty to, go farther in protecting the common good by obliging his subjects to use due diligence lest the common good be injured.[24]

The second basis, then, for imputing acts as criminal is negligence.[25] Criminal negligence is properly imputable to the delinquent since he has an obligation to avoid violating the law. The criminal act is not directly willed, but it is willed indirectly through the wilful failure to avoid injuring the common good. Criminal negligence is the

[22] Canon 2200, § 1—"Dolis heic est deliberata voluntas violandi legem, eique opponitur ex parte intellectus defectus cognitionis et ex parte voluntatis defectus libertatis."

[23] Canon 2200, § 2—"Posita externa legis violatione, dolus in foro externo praesumitur, donec contrarium probetur." Cf. also Regatillo, II, 448; Wernz-Vidal, VII, 62.

[24] Michiels, I, 106.

[25] Canon 2199—"Imputabilitas delicti pendet ex dolo delinquentis vel ex eiusdem culpa in ignorantia legis violatae aut in omissione debitae diligentiae; . . ."

morally imputable neglect to avoid committing a criminal act,[26] and is to be found either in a culpable ignorance of the law violated, or in the omission of due diligence.[27]

Canon 2199 explicitly indicates two forms of criminal negligence: culpable ignorance of the law violated, and the culpable omission of due diligence. A crime committed through ignorance of the law is imputed to the delinquent when he has culpably failed to consider the illegality of his act. A crime committed through the omission of due diligence is imputed to the delinquent because he did not trouble to foresee the evil effects flowing from his action, or foreseeing them, did not trouble to avert them.[28]

Ignorance of the law is the lack of knowledge concerning the existence, nature, or comprehension of the law.[29] Such ignorance may be negative, insofar as the delinquent had no knowledge of the law; positive, insofar as he made an erroneous judgment concerning the law's existence or comprehension; or simple inadvertence.[30] The precise effect of ignorance upon imputability will be discussed in the following chapter. The ignorance may be such as will take away, or such as will only diminish, the degree of culpability.

The criminal act *is* directly intended when the crime is committed in ignorance of the law, but the violation of the law is not directly intended. In crimes resulting from omission of due diligence, the act done *is not* directly criminal nor is it willed directly.[31]

Several possible situations may result from the performance of an action which has several effects, some of which are criminal. If the criminal effects cannot be foreseen, or, if foreseen, cannot in any way be avoided, the

[26] "Culpa in genere est negligentia moraliter imputabilis evitandi effectum crimiosum."—Regatillo, II, 448. Cf. Conorata, IV, 26.

[27] Canon 2199.

[28] Michiels, I, 107.

[29] Wernz-Vidal, VII, 69.

[30] Wernz-Vidal, VII, 69; Michiels, I, 107-108.

[31] Michiels, I, 108.

agent is certainly not guilty of any crime. The criminal effects cannot in any manner be attributed to the agent, and hence no criminal imputability is possible.[32]

The criminal effects may be foreseen, but at the same time may be avoidable only at the price of not doing the action at all. If the agent has a right to do the act, then he is free to do so in spite of some criminal effects which will follow. The criminal effects will not be imputed to him, since they are not in any way intended by him, nor can he impede them except by giving up his legitimate right to act.[33]

Finally, the agent may be able, through the use of due diligence, both to foresee the criminal effects, and also to avoid them. Then he is bound to do so. To perform the action without avoiding the criminal effects will cause them to be imputed to him. It makes no difference whether the agent actually did foresee the criminal effects or not. If he could and should have foreseen them, and could have avoided them through due diligence but did not, he is guilty of criminal negligence.[34]

To impute criminal effects to an agent by reason of his lack of due diligence, the following conditions must be verified:

(1) The criminal effects must arise from the action or omission of the agent as from their efficient cause, and

(2) The agent must have been able to foresee and to impede the criminal effects of his action.[35]

Article II. Responsibility for Civil Crimes

Section 1. Civil Law and the Moral Order

In the centuries before the Reformation, all of Europe was united in the profession of one common faith. Truth

[32] Michiels, I, 109.

[33] Michiels, I, 109.

[34] Michiels, I, 110; Regatillo, II, 448.

[35] Michiels, I, 110-111.

was looked upon as one, and the principles of morality as laid down by faith and reason were guiding norms for all men of whatever station. The law governing the external actions of men in the State were governed by the law of that land, but even the law of the land was within the framework of the general principles of the moral order.

The English common law developed with little dependence upon the systems of law in vogue on the Continent. Then English kings lived and ruled, *sub Deo et sub lege,* subject to God and to the law. The king was subject to the divine law, whether positive or natural, and was not free to rule his people in violation of their God-given rights. Like every other citizen the king was also subject to the law of the land.

Much of the life of the citizen of England was controlled by the ecclesiastical courts. Questions of marriage, wills and inheritance, clerical life, etc., were controlled by the canon law and not by the common law. There has been much discussion whether this canon law was proper to England, or whether it was the common law of the Universal Church.

From the time of the Reformation it became customary to say that the Church of England had always chosen whatever of the Roman Church canon law it wished, and that it was only through such an adoption that it became the law of the ecclesiastical courts. In 1883 a Commission on Ecclesiastical Courts was bold enough to make the following bald statement:

> But the canon law of Rome, although always regarded as of great authority in England, was not held to be binding on the courts.[36]

This proposition was first seriously attacked by Sir William Maitland (1850-1906) in his series of essays collected in a work entitled *Roman Canon Law in the Church of England,* published in London in 1898. The reputation

[36] *Report of the Ecclesiastical Courts Commission, 1883,* Vol. I (London, 1883), p. xviii.

of this renowned scholar in the history of law was enough to set off a veritable torrent of argumentation. In 1931 Z. N. Brooke of the University of Cambridge published the result of his study of the manuscripts and documents of medieval England in regard to the force of canon law during the medieval period. He concluded, with Maitland, that the common law of the Roman Church did govern much of the civil life of England:

> We are accustomed to hear that the English Church selected from the canons of the Roman Church such as it thought fit to accept. If so, some record must have been kept of that selection, or no one would have known what law to follow. We should expect to find several manuscripts of it. On the contrary, there is not the slightest trace of a special collection selected for the use of the English Church in any manuscript, in any medieval library catalogue, in any contemporary writer. Clearly it did not exist. The English Church was subject to the same laws, to all the same laws, that the rest of the Church obeyed.[37]

Two systems of jurisprudence ruled in England, common law and canon law. Between these two systems there was much borrowing and inter-play; the independence of the common law from all other systems of law should not be overemphasized. The common law could not offer all the remedies that the principles of justice demanded and there grew up the supplementary and equitable jurisdiction of the Lord Chancellor. The principles applied in this civil court were those of the Roman Law and those of the Canon Law, which itself was based on Roman Law. The chancellors in the medieval ages were almost inevitably bishops, who had been trained as canon lawyers, and in the Roman Law.[38] Their influence upon the common

[37] Brooke, *The English Church and the Papacy from the Conquest to the Reign of John* (Cambridge: The University Press, 1931), p. 99.

[38] Hughes, *The Reformation in England* (3 vols., London: Hollis & Carter, 1950-1954), I, 73 (hereafter cited as Hughes).

law was more in the manner of checking abuses than in that of a direct formation.

The practice of using, in the civil service of the king, clerics who had been trained in canon law was a common one throughout the middle ages. Education was accessible for the cleric, and the king often found it convenient to use him in the king's service. It was a source of income to the cleric and often the means of rising higher in ecclesiastical circles. Moorman in his work on the Church in the thirteenth century notes this fact, and felt that it was of detriment to the Church:

> Finally, there were those who, either from inclination or from the desire to augment their slender incomes, engaged in secular occupation unbecoming to the cloth.... Some made use of their abilities and education by obtaining posts such as bailiffs and seneschals, while others engaged in the work of the courts, acting as proctors, advocates and assessors. In 1293 Bishop Pontissara wrote to the Rector of Sanderstead citing him to answer various charges, among which was one that he had acted as advocate and judge in a secular court.[39]

Throughout the fourteenth century and up to the time of the Reformation this practice continued. The king relied more and more upon clerics to be his ambassadors, councilors, and civil servants. As Pantin notes, this was also a rather sure manner of rising to the rank of a bishop, for the recommendation of the king was of great weight in Rome.[40]

All of these factors tended to keep the common law within the framework of the principles of the moral order. The king himself was subject to God, and hence was bound to legislate according to the law of God in regard to man's actions. The influence of the ecclesiastical courts upon much of the life of the country upheld this principle that the law

[39] Moorman, *Church Life in England in the Thirteenth Century* (Cambridge: At the University Press, 1955), p. 150.

[40] Pantin, *The English Church in the Fourteenth Century* (Cambridge: At the Universitiy Press, 1955), p. 11.

was only one part of the moral order before all who dealt with the law. The common use of clerics, trained in canon law, as judges, counselors, chancellors, and ambassadors of the king was a strong influence for unity in the philosophy of law, at least in fundamental principles.

Following the Reformation, the study of civil law became divorced from theological moral principles and came to be established as a science of its own with its own guiding norms. When King Henry VIII (1509-1547) ended the study of canon law in England, he established chairs of civil law in the Universities to fulfill his needs.[41] This marked the separation of the civil law and the canon law in matters of fundamental principles. English civil law, and the American civil law which is its heir, drifted slowly from the guiding influence of theological moral principles, and established themselves as independent sciences receiving their fundamental norms from no other source than humanistic philosophy, if that.

SECTION 2. CIVIL LAW MEANING OF CRIMINAL INTENT

In the Anglo-American system of jurisprudence, the commission of a forbidden act, or the omission of a commanded act, will not, of itself, suffice for the commission of a crime. There must also be the operation of the intellect and the free will of the agent. Motive, the reason why one intends to violate the law, is not part of the criminal intent. The concept of criminal intent is limited to the judgment of the intellect, followed by the command of the free will that this particular violation of the law is to be performed.

Blackstone saw the intimate connection between the activity of the will and reward or punishment. If the agent is not the moral cause, but only the physical cause, of his action, he cannot earn any reward or punishment:

> An involuntary act, as it has no claim to merit, so neither can it induce guilt. To make a com-

[41] Hughes, I, 74.

> plete crime cognizable by human laws, there must be both a will and an act.[42]

Modern American jurisprudence insists just as strongly as did Blackstone upon the place of the will in the commission of a crime. Without such inner responsibility there can be no criminal responsibility. Burdick states this as an essential element of criminal justice:

> In addition to an act, a mental element, variously called "the will," "the intent," "the evil intent," "the guilty mind," and "the criminal intent," is necessary to constitute a crime. This is an inherent requirement of justice, since to punish one for an act for which he was in no way mentally responsible would be a denial of all justice.[43]

If the criminal act is done not by the command of the will, but from such a compelling outside force that the will is not free to act, there can be no such thing as a crime. It is not possible to label as criminal those acts which are purely involuntary, as reflex actions, or those acts which are done under such force or fear that the freedom of action is taken away. As Burdick says:

> The criminal law deals only with voluntary acts, things done in obedience to the will.[44]

Before the will can come into action, there must be reflection on the part of the intellect. The intellect must know what is being done. Lack of mental capacity, as in children or among the insane, takes away the possibility of committing a crime. The use of reason is essential before the will can command a criminal act.

> In criminal law, intent means a state of mind which willingly consents to the act that is done, or free will, choice, or volition in the doing of an act. It means that the act is voluntary, that it proceeds from a mind free to act in distinction from an act done without mental capacity to understand its nature, or under circumstances

[42] Blackstone, IV, 14.

[43] Burdick, I, 122-3; Duncan *vs.* State, 7 Humph. (Tenn.) 148 (1846).

[44] Burdick, I, 106.

> which sufficiently show that it was the result of involuntary forces and against the will.[45]

SECTION 3. THE PROBLEM OF MENS REA

Scholars may disagree as to whether the primitive jurisprudence of Anglo-Saxon England considered the question of personal guilt in inflicting punishment for crime,[46] but certainly after the coming of William the Conqueror (1066-1087) the concept of *mens rea* was part of the law.[47] The laws of King Henry II (1154-1189) quoted the legal maxim, *Actus non est reus, nisi mens sit rea,*[48] and such famous writers as Lord Coke (1552-1634) often referred to it.

Blackstone insisted upon a vicious will as being necessary for the constituting of a crime. It was as wrong to punish a vicious act without a vicious will, as it would be to have the civil courts try to punish the vicious will without any overt act. His words are clear:

> And, as a vicious will without a vicious act is no civil crime, so, on the other hand, an unwarrantable act without a vicious will is no crime at all.

[45] Burdick, I, 126.

[46] Pro: Mueller, "Crime, Tort and the Primitive," *The Journal of Criminal Law, Criminology and Police Science* (Chicago, Ill.: Northwestern University School of Law, 1910—),XLVI (1955), 303 ff.; contra: Sayre, "The Present Significance of *Mens Rea,*" *Harvard Legal Essays* (Cambridge, Mass.: Harvard University Press, 1934), pp. 399 ff.

[47] "Monks and scholars trained in Roman and Canon Law imported the Roman form of *mens rea,* namely *dolus* and *culpa,* or intent and negligence to England."—Mueller, *"Mens Rea," West Virginia Law Review* (Morgantown, W. Va.: West Virginia Univ.), LVIII (1955), 34.

[48] *Leges Henrici,* 5, sec. 28. Pollock and Maitland (*History of English Law* (2. ed., 2 vols., Cambridge: At the University Press, 1909), II 476) held that Henry got the maxim from the *Decretum Gratiani* c. 3, C. 22, q. 2. The quotation is from Chapter 2 of Sermon 180 of St. Augustine, which has reference only to perjury. The words are: "*Ream linguam non facit nisi mens rea.*" It was commonly found in canonical collections of the Middle Ages, and Henry could have taken it from Ivo's *Pandects,* VIII, 111, Ivo's *Decretum,* XII, 39, or from the *Collectio Trium Partium,* III, 22.

> So that to constitute a crime against human laws, there must be, first, a vicious will; and secondly, an unlawful act consequent upon such vicious will.[49]

Consistent with this inheritance, many modern writers still insist upon the guilty mind as an essential element of criminal intent. In *American Jurisprudence* we find this statement:

> Under the common law a crime consists of two elements—namely an evil intention and an unlawful action. *"Actus non facit reum, nisi mens sit rea"* in the words of the maxim. A crime is not committed if the mind of the person doing the unlawful act is innocent; a guilty intention is essential.[50]

Before entering upon a discussion of the state of the doctrine of *mens rea* in American law today, it is essential to separate the concept of motive from that of guilty knowledge, or the criminal mind. Motive is the reason why a man acts. John Doe may know that arson is against the law, and yet burns down his neighbor's house to enable his neighbor to collect the insurance money which the neighbor needs to pay medical bills. His motive—to help his neighbor—is a good one, but he intends to violate the law. John Doe has the criminal mind, or *mens rea.* The law is not concerned with motive, but with intent.[51]

Modern American jurisprudence has made great inroads upon the doctrine of *mens rea.* The whole question is in such a state of confusion that Burdick does not hesitate to write: "There is no general agreement as to what *mens rea* means."[52] The growth of absolute liability statutes has caused much confusion in the whole law.

[49] Blackstone, IV, 14.

[50] 14 Am. Jur. Crim. Law 23.

[51] "The intent applies to and qualifies the act. Motive is the propelling power which leads to the act. And while it is essential in common law crimes that an intent to commit the crime should appear, either expressly or by implication, no such necessity exists as to motive, and it need not be proved."—May, P. 17. Cf. U.S. *vs.* Harmon, 45 Fed. 414 (1891).

[52] Burdick, I, 162.

The first breach of the wall was probably in the statutory rape statutes. In order to protect the public morals, it was felt necessary to legislate out of existence any criminal mind in the cases of sexual intercourse with women of tender years. Thus in the case of Brown *vs.* State, the defendant was indicted and found guilty of statutory rape for having immoral relations with a girl under eighteen years of age. There was no question of force or even of lack of consent on the part of the girl. The defendant pleaded the doctrine of *mens rea.* The defendant did not know that the girl was under eighteen years of age, since she appeared to be much older, and thus the defendant had reason to believe that she was of age. The court[53] held the defendant to absolute liability and sustained the conviction of rape.

The rise of statutes imposing absolute liability for their mere violation without reference to knowledge or *mens rea* has been great. A number of these referring to impure food, milk control, selling of liquor to minors, drugs, and oleomargerine have been cited in footnote 38 of Chapter II at page 28. The North Carolina Supreme Court has stated explicitly that even an honest mistake will not be considered as a defense in these statutory crimes.

> A positive wilful intent, as distinguished from a mere "intent" to violate the criminal law is not an essential ingredient of crime. This is especially true in statutory offenses (*mala prohibita*). The law implies conclusively the "guilty intent," although the defendant was honestly mistaken.[54]

The Supreme Court of the United States, too, has not been silent on the growth or existence of crimes that do not include any requisite of the guilty mind. Chief Justice Vinson (1890-1953) perhaps saw the rule of American Law as including the concept of *mens rea,* but the rule suffered notable exceptions. In the case of U.S. *vs.* Dennis, he wrote:

[53] Brown *vs.* State, 23 Del. 159, 74 Atl. 836 (1909).

[54] State *vs.* McBrayer, 98 N.C. 619, 2 S.E. 755, (1887).

> A survey of Title 18 of the U.S. Code indicates that the vast majority of the crimes designated by that title require, by express language, proof of the existence of a certain mental state, in words such as "knowingly," "maliciously," "wilfully," "with the purpose of," "with the intent to," or combinations or permutations of these and synonymous terms. The existence of a *mens rea* is the rule of, rather than the exception to, the principles of Anglo-American criminal jurisprudence.[55]

The law books of America are growing fat with statutory legislation necessary to govern the increasingly complex civilization in which we live. The major part of our criminal law is now statutory, and most of it does not include any conception of the doctrine of *mens rea.* Mistake of fact or law no longer can be pleaded as a defense to much of our criminal law. Ignorance of the law, no matter how numerous and complicated these laws may be, is no excuse. Thus it is that Mueller could write:

> The rule has developed that in all regulatory penal law mistake of fact is no defense. Thus, the ancient and sacrosanct maxim of common law, *actus non facit reum nisi mens est rea,* has been abrogated in a major part of penal law today.[56]

The state of mind of the criminal is of no interest to the courts once it has settled the question of voluntariness. If the act has been done freely by the delinquent, then he has committed a crime. In summing up this principle, Burdick did not hesitate to express the doctrine in such clear terms that no one can mistake its applicability to concrete cases. He wrote:

> However, intent in the meaning of criminal law is present in all cases when the act is done voluntarily or willingly, that is, through no compulsion or lack of mental capacity. Granting that one may act in ignorance, that an act was not done with an intention to disobey the law or to commit

[55] U.S.*vs*. Dennis, 341 U.S. 494, 95 L. Ed. 1137, 71 S.S. 857 (1951).
[56] Mueller, p. 38.

> any wrong, granting further that the accused would not have done the act had he known the truth, nevertheless, he had freedom of action, the power of choice, and therefore his act was voluntary, or in other words, intentional in a legal sense.[57]

One must use great caution in determining the role of *mens rea* in any given crime in American jurisprudence. In those jurisdictions where the common law is still in effect, common law crimes will generally still have a true *mens rea* as part of the definition of the crime. If the common law crimes have been reduced to a code, then one must examine the statutes to see if the wording includes any requirement of *mens rea.*

SECTION 4. THE PRESUMPTION OF INTENT

There is a presumption of law that a man intends to do those things which he has done, and that he intends their consequences. Thus a criminal act leads to the presumption that the agent intended to violate the law. Burdick states it in these terms:

> It is a presumption of law that one intends the necessary and natural consequences of his voluntary act, and a deliberate and unlawful act gives rise to a presumption of malice or intent. . . .[58]

This presumption is subject to rebuttal, but even the refutation will be of no avail in the absolute liability statutes.

It is clear that the results of the act must be such as would naturally rise from the action. We thus see the approach to criminal negligence with its foreseeability requisite. One is held for the natural consequences of his acts, and not for things which would not naturally flow therefrom. A man can be held for the bloody nose he causes in striking another, but not for the fact that the

[57] Burdick, I, 159.

[58] Burdick, I, 136; State *vs.* Mills, 6 Penn. (Del.) 497, 69 Atl. 841 (1908); Com. *vs.* Hawkins, 157 Mass. 551, 32 N.E. 862 (1893).

blood falling on the man's hand caused an irritation which became infected, and later caused death.

In all cases of criminal negligence, it is a basic premise that the criminal act was not directly intended. The agent intended, indeed, to do what he did, but did not intend the criminal results which he could and should have foreseen. The criminal acts, however, are actually intended in the legal sense. This doctrine is expounded by Burdick in these words:

> The causalities or consequences which may result from negligence are not usually intended in the sense that they are wilfully planned or preconceived, but the negligence itself is voluntary and therefore intended in the legal sense.[59]

The law may impose a duty upon its citizens to act in a given set of circumstances. Registration for the draft is a common example in recent decades in the United States. Failure to comply with these laws results in a legal injury that is criminal. The law is violated in the instance both of non-action by deliberate will, and of non-action by negligence. May discusses this point, and sums up in these words:

> Where the duty of acting exists, negligence, resulting in an injury that the law punishes, will make the defendant responsible for that injury.[60]

Citizens have many obligations to act which flow from law, contract, or from their own will. No matter what the source of their action, they must perform their acts in such a way as to avoid injuring others and the common good. If the negligence in action is such as to constitute a criminal offense, they are guilty of crime by negligence.

> Any duty which one undertakes ought to be so performed as not to injure the public, and negligence in the performance of any duty, if its re-

[59] Burdick, I, 138; see Stein *vs.* State, 37 Ala. 125 (1861); Green *vs.* State, 150 *Ga.* 121, 102 S.E. 813 (1920); Pool *vs.* State, 87 Ga. 526, 13 S.E. 556 (1891); State *vs.* Moore, 129 Iowa 514, 106 N.W. 16 (1906); Peay *vs.* Com., 181 Ky. 396 205 S.W. 404 (1918); Com. *vs.* Hawkins, 157 Mass. 551, 32 N.E. 862 (1893).

[60] May, p. 24.

sult is in its nature criminal, ought to be punished.[61]

In attempting to define that negligence which will be criminal, the courts have used many expressions such as culpable, gross, wicked, criminal, complete, clear, reckless, careless. Such terms always imply the concepts of foreseeability, and preventability. If the act is criminal, was foreseeable, and likewise preventable, it is criminal negligence so to act.[62]

The definition of some individual crime may contain in itself elements other than those which are common to all crimes. There can be no crime without criminal intent understood as a voluntary doing of the act, but other factors may be added as requisite. The individual statute must be studied, but a few of these added requisites deserve special mention.

Malice is an element applicable only to those crimes which contain mention of some element of deliberation or purpose in their very definition. In such crimes as arson, libel, mayhem and malicious mischief, the criminal has such a hardness of heart that he is performing the act with knowledge of the evil consequences.[63] Malice always looks to the mental state of the agent as its chief concern, and since the mental state of an arsonist is different from that of one who commits libel, the term malice will have different meanings in different crimes. It is present in every deliberate crime, even if not required by law for that crime.[64]

[61] May, p. 24; State *vs.* O'Brien, 32 N.J. L. 169 (1867).

[62] "The natural consequences of one's acts are presumed to be intended by Him and a negligent performance or omission of legal duty is proper evidence of intent unless a specific intent is required." —Burdick, I, 137.

[63] "Criminal intent is an element of all crimes, but malice is properly applied only to deliberate acts done on purpose and with design."—Burdick, I, 132.

[64] "In law, with the possible exception of malicious mischief, it is always subjective, never objective, and refers merely to the state or condition of one's mind when doing a criminal act. It includes

CHAPTER IV

CAUSES AFFECTING IMPUTABILITY

ARTICLE I. IN ECCLESIASTICAL CRIMINAL LAW

The free will of the agent is the basis for imputing crimes to their author. If the author of an action is not free, the action he performs is not properly his, and he should receive neither merit nor blame for it. Man's will, however, is a blind faculty, and must have knowledge before it can act.[1] If an action is to have any moral value, its author must have the requisite fore-knowledge of its rightness or wrongness. Whatever affects the operation of the intellect or the will, affects the degree of imputability of the crime. Canon 2199 states the principle that anything that increases, diminishes, or takes away the malice or criminal negligence will, by that very fact, increase, diminish, or take away the imputability of the crime.[2]

Certain causes take away completely the use of the intellect and/or the will. If such a cause is present, an essential requisite for imputability is destroyed, and all imputability is taken away. Some of these causes are presumed in law to be present, e.g., infancy, with no regard to their actual effect upon the intellect or will. Others, such as ignorance or passion, come into play only by reason of their actual effect upon the intellect or will. The principle of law is given in canon 2201, § 1, which states that those who lack the use of reason are incapable of crime. The canon reads:

[1] "There cannot be any question of a deliberate and free act, and consequently, also, of any free anti-juridical act, unless there was previous knowledge on the part of the agent."—Swoboda, p. 88.

[2] Canon 2199—"...quare omnes causae quae augent, minuunt, tollunt dolum aut culpam, eo ipso augent, minuunt, tollunt delicti imputabilitatem."

Delicti sunt incapaces qui actu carent usu rationis.

In other cases the intellect and the will may be able to function, but their processes are so interfered with by some particular cause that less than full consent and full deliberation has accompanied the act. If such interfering factors are proved to the satisfaction of the judge is an ecclesiastical trial, the imputability of the crime is diminished.

Surrounding every crime are the particular circumstances of each given crime. Some of these circumstances may take away or diminish the imputability of the crime; others may add to the imputability of the crime. If a circumstance changes the very nature of the crime and turns it into another species of crime, the circumstance does not increase the imputability, since this was included in the very definition of the crime itself. Consideration is given here only to those circumstances which do not change the species of the crime, but simply are attendant as accidental features, and thus increase or diminish imputability.

SECTION 1. AGE

An infant is defined in canon 88, § 3, as one who has not completed the seventh year of age. As a presumption of law, infants are held not to possess the use of reason.[3] This is not to imply that one who is legally an infant is incapable of sin. If he has the use of reason and wilfully violates the law, he sins before God and his own conscience. The lack of mental capacity in an infant is a juridical presumption, and does not look to the actual facts.

An application of this presumption can be found in canon 12, which states that those who have not yet completed their seventh year of age are not bound by purely ecclesiastical laws.[4] The canon specifically considers that

[3] Canon 88, § 3—"Impubes, ante plenum septennium, dicitur infans seu puer vel parvulus et censetur non sui compos;..."

[4] Canon 12—"Legibus mere ecclesiasticis non tenentur qui baptismum non receperunt, nec baptizati qui sufficienti rationis usu non

such infants may possess the use of reason, but states nevertheless that they are not subject to the law. Since penal laws are purely ecclesiastical laws, no infant can have an action imputed to him as criminal.[5] The possibility of holding an infant for a crime which violates the divine and ecclesiastical law is so remote that it is seldom treated by the authors.[6]

A minor in ecclesiastical law is a person who has not completed his twenty-first year of age.[7] The presumption is made in the law that a person of minor age will not have the full and mature use of his intellect, or the full control of his will. The nearer he is in age to infancy, the more reason there is to presume that the delinquent has less control over his intellect and will. Thus the law states that unless the contrary is evident, minor age does diminish the imputability of crimes.[8]

As Roberti points out, this is a simple presumption of law and is subject to rebuttal. Hence a judge can hold that the minor age of a particular delinquent in no way affected his reason or will, and that full imputability of the crime is to be attributed to him.[9] The law, in canon 2230, contains an exception to this presumption when it states that those who have attained the age of puberty do incure the penalties stated in the law if they either induce another to violate the law, or concur in the com-

gaudent, *nec qui, licet rationis usum assecuti, septimum aetatis annum nondum expleverunt*, nisi aliud iure expresse caveatur." (Italics supplied by writer.)

[5] Wernz-Vidal, VII, 86; Roberti, I, 112; Regatillo, II, 454: "Quodsi in casu particulari illa praesumptio non verificatur, licet factum contra legem ecclesiasticam vel divinam moraliter sit imputabile et peccatum, responsabilitatem poenalem infantes non incurrunt, cum responsabilitas poenalis per legem ecclesiasticam inducatur, qua etiam in tali casu non tenetur."

[6] Michiels, I, 145.

[7] Canon 88, § 1—"Persona quae vicesimum primum aetatis annum explevit, maior est; infra hanc aetatem, minor."

[8] Canon 2204—"Minor aetas, nisi aliud constet, minuit delicti imputabilitatem eoque magis quo ad infantiam propius accedit."

[9] Roberti, I, 112; Michiels, I, 146, 147.

mission of a delict in the manner stated in canon 2209, §§ 1-3.

SECTION 2. MENTAL DISTURBANCES

The ecclesiastical law governing those who are habiutally insane is found in canon 2201, § 2. Those who are habitually insane, although they have lucid intervals, or in certain processes of reasoning or of acting are sane, are nevertheless presumed incapable of committing a crime.[10] Ecclesiastical law does not give a definition of sanity which could help one in determining who are habitually insane. The science of mental disturbances is not the province of the law, but the object of the science of medicine.[11]

The ecclesiastical law will use experts in the science of mental health to give their professional opinions regarding the mental condition of the defendant.[12] The proper use of these experts is governed by the procedure found in canons 1792 to 1805. The judge is not bound to adopt the conclusions of the experts, even if they are unanimous. He must take into consideration all the facts and circumstances.[13] In handing down his decision, the judge is bound to that degree of moral certitude which is required by canon 1869 for the pronouncement of any sentence.

The law gives the principles to be applied once the question of habitual insanity has been settled by the court through the use of experts. A presumption of law arises that such persons who are habitually insane are incapa-

[10] Canon 2201, § 2—"Habitualiter amentes, licet quandoque lucida intervalla habeant, vel in certis quibusdam ratiocinationibus vel actibus sani videantur, delicti tamen incapaces praesumuntur."

[11] Michiels, I, 154: "Studium harum perturbationum mentalium . . . constituit proprium scientiae psychiatricae objectum."

[12] Michiels, I, 154: ". . . ideoque, quando in casu quodam concreto de responsabilitate criminali delinquentis mentaliter alienati, perturbati aut debilitati ferenda est sententia, regulariter psychiatriae peritorum judicium est invocandum."

[13] Canon 1804, § 1—"Iudex non peritorum tantum conclusiones, etsi concordes, sed cetera quoque causae adiuncta attente perpendat."

ble of committing a crime. It makes no difference that they do have lucid intervals, or that they are rational on some issues.

It is the common opinion of canonists that the presumption which receives mention in canon 2201, § 2, in regard to the habitually insane is a simple presumption of law.[14] Such presumptions are subject to rebuttal by direct or indirect proof.[15] If the crime has been committed during a lucid interval, this must be proved to the court before the defendant can be found guilty of the crime.[16] It should be noted that he who has the benefit of a presumption is free from all burden of proof.[17] It would be the office of the promoter of justice to carry the burden of proving that the action was performed during a lucid interval.

Weakness of mind diminishes, but does not take away, the imputability of a crime.[18] Under the expression weakness of mind, may be included all pathological mental states and all psychic factors which will not take away, but will interfere with, the freedom of the action of the will of the delinquent.[19] Weakness of mind due to old age is commonly included.[20]

It is for the judge to determine the degree of imputability in those who suffer from weakness of mind. In coming to a decision, one will most appropriately have recourse to the testimony of experts in these matters, and hear

[14] Michiels, I, 172; Vermeersch-Creusen, *Epitome Iuris Canonici* (6. ed., 3 vols., Mechliniae-Romae: H. Desssain, 1937-1946), III, 226 (hereafter cited as Vermeersch-Creusen).

[15] Canon 1826—"Contra praesumptionem iuris simpliciter admittitur probatio tum directa tum indirecta;..."

[16] Michiels, I, 172; Vermeesch-Creusen, III, 226: "Mera praesumptio statuitur; quare legibus poenalibus inter lucida intervalla vel in iis materiis in quibus non desipiunt tenenter."

[17] Canon 1827—"Qui habet pro se iuris praesumptionem, liberatur ab onere probandi, quod recidit in partem adversam;..."

[18] Canon 2201, § 4—"Debilitas mentis delicti imputabilitatem minuit, sed non tollit omnino."

[19] Abbo-Hannon, II, 789; Michiels, I, 177.

[20] Vermeersch-Creusen, III, 228.

witnesses who have observed the conduct of the delinquent in the past. The exact determination of the various mental states which will affect the freedom of the will is one for the psychological and medical profession.[21]

SECTION 3. DRUNKENNESS, DRUGS, SLEEP

Consistent with the general principle enunciated in paragraph one of canon 2201, the third paragraph of this same canon states that involuntary complete drunkenness, if it takes away completely the use of reason, will also take away all imputability for crimes committed in such a state of drunkenness.[22] The discussion turns here not upon the moral or social aspects of drunkenness, but upon the effect of drunkenness on the mind, and hence on imputability.

Involuntary and perfect drunkenness will excuse the defendant from responsibility for his act. The criminal act was performed without the use of reason; hence there is no direct causality between the will of the agent and the act. The defendant is not even indirectly responsible for the act, since the drunkenness was completely involuntary.[23] Neither directly nor indirectly can the criminal act be said to flow from the will of the agent; criminal imputability is completely taken away.

The last sentence in canon 2201, § 3, applies the same principles there used with reference to complete drunkenness to other like disturbances of the mind.[24] The use of cocaine, morphine, opium and like drugs would have the same effect upon imputability if their use was involun-

[21] See Roberti, I, 114; Michiels, I, 177.

[22] Canon 2201, § 3—"...violata autem lege in ebrietate involuntaria, imputabilitas exsulat omnino, si ebrietas usum rationis adimat ex toto;..."

[23] Regatillo, II, 451; Wernz-Vidal, VII, 95: "Perfecta et involuntaria excludit delicti imputabilitatem in ea commissi; tum in se, ob defectum cognitionis in actu delicti; tum in causa, ob defectum voluntaria in ebrietate contrahenda."

[24] Canon 2201, § 3—"Idem dicatur de aliis similibus mentis perturbationibus."

tary, and had the effect of taking away the use of reason.[25] In this same category must be placed other involuntary conditions of the mind which take away the use of reason, such as sleep, hynosis, etc. If the condition is not voluntary and was so complete as to take away the use of reason, there can be no imputability for crimes committed by a person while in such a state.[26]

Crimes committed while one is voluntarily drunk do not lose their imputability, but they are to be imputed to the delinquent in a lesser degree than are crimes which are committed while he is in full control of his faculties. These are two exceptions to this general principle: if the drunkenness was voluntarily brought on for the purpose of committing the crime, or if the drunkenness was induced in order to have an excuse from the punishment. These principles apply also to other disturbances of the mind which are voluntarily induced, such as result from the use of drugs, hypnotism, etc.[27]

Since the delinquent is responsible for his drunkenness, he is responsible, at least *in causa,* for the crimes which he may commit during his voluntary drunkenness. Thus the voluntarily drunken delinquent cannot be absolved from the responsibility for his crimes. The law does, however, recognize a lessening of the imputability of the crime, since the crime was willed not in itself, but only indirectly by reason of the delinquent's having willed the drunkenness. It is for this reason that there is some lessening of the imputability.[28]

[25] Vermeersch-Creusen, III, 226.

[26] Regatillo, II, 451; Wernz-Vidal, VII, 92; Michiels, I, 151.

[27] Canon 2201, § 3—"Delictum in ebrietate voluntaria commissum aliqua imputabilitate non vacat, sed ea minor est quam cum idem delictum committitur ab eo qui sui plene compos sit, nisi tamen ebrietas apposite ad delictum patrandum vel excusandum quaesita sit; violata autem lege in ebrietate involuntaria, imputabilitas exsulat omnino, si ebrietas usum rationis adimat ex toto; minuitur, si ex parte tantum. Idem dicatur de aliis similibus mentis perturbationibus."

[28] Michiels, I, 173-176; Roberti, I, 115, 116.

It is apparent at once why the law makes the two exceptions to the general principle. If the delinquent renders himself drunk for the purpose of committing the crime, or in order to use the drunkenness as an excuse, he is directly willing the commission of the crime. It cannot be said that the drunkenness alone was directly willed, and the crime was willed only indirectly.[29]

If the drunkenness was not voluntary, but likewise did not take away completely the use of reason, the delinquent is to be held responsible for the crime. The degree of imputability of the crime is lessened, since there was not a full control over the will which commanded the crime.

The precise degree of the lessened imputability must be determined by the judge. It is his role to evaluate the testimony of the witnesses and the experts, and, from these, to draw conclusions as to the degree of responsibility of the delinquent.[30]

SECTION 4. IGNORANCE AND MISTAKE

The violation of laws that are not known by the defendant is not a crime if the ignorance was in no way culpable.[31] This principle, simply stated, means that ignorance of the law is an excuse if the ignorance is not the fault of the agent. The principle flows naturally from the definition of a crime as a morally imputable violation of the law.

Ignorance is the privation of knowledge in a subject naturally capable of it.[32] There is a lack or an absence of that which should be present, to wit, knowledge. It is

[29] Wernz-Vidal, VII, 95.

[30] Canon 2218.

[31] Canon 2202, § 1—"Violatio legis ignoratae nullatenus imputatur, si ignorantia fuerit inculpabilis; . . ."

[32] St. Thomas Aquinas, *Summa Theologica,* I-II, q. 76, art. 2: "Ignorantia vero importat scientiae privationem: dum scilicet alicui deest scientia eorum quae natus est scire." See also Wernz-Vidal, VII, 97.

only by analogy that one speaks of ignorance in animals or of ignorance in material things. A privation can be predicated only of an object which should possess that which is not present.[33] In considering the effect of ignorance upon imputability, the canonist prescinds completely from all except those who enjoy the use of reason, and hence could have known of the law or the fact in question.

The fundamentals of criminal imputability must be found either in malice or in criminal negligence. Since knowledge and ignorance are mutually exclusive, it is not possible for malice to serve as the foundation for the imputing of crimes when the agent was in ignorance. Criminal negligence is the font from which springs the will's part in committing a crime when the intellect was in ignorance.

The criminal law of the Church requires moral imputability before there can be legal imputability. If the lack of knowledge is in no way the fault of the agent, it cannot be imputed to him morally, and hence there is no legal fault. Such ignorance is known as invincible ignorance. When invincible ignorance is present there can be no sin,[34] and without moral imputability there can be no ecclesiastical crime.[35]

Jurists often speak of ignorance of the law and ignorance of the fact. The distinction between these is simple and clear. Ignorance of the law has reference to the existence or applicability of the law; ignorance of the fact has reference to the nature or the effects of the action being performed. Swoboda has expressed the distinction very clearly:

> If the existence, extent or meaning of the law is not known there is ignorance of law. If the concrete or physical conditions necessary for the

[33] Swoboda, p. 116. This dissertation offers an excellent and exhaustive treatment of the whole question of ignorance in regard to criminal imputability.

[34] St. Thomas Aquinas, I-II, q. 76, art. 2: "...nulla ignorantia invincibilis est peccatum;..."

[35] Swoboda, pp. 154-157.

application of the law are not known there is ignorance of fact.[36]

Besides these two distinctions, there is ignorance simply of the penalty. Here there is no ignorance of the existence or extent of the law, or of the concrete act's being a violation of the law; there is ignorance simply of the attaching of a penalty to a given violation of the law.

The ignorance noted in canon 2202, § 1, can be ignorance either of the law or of the fact. When one acts in ignorance of the law, one intends indeed to do the act which one performs, but one is excused from culpability because of this ignorance. If the ignorance was of the fact, then the agent did not know the nature of what he was doing, or its consequences, and cannot be held responsible for them under the criminal law.[37]

Ignorance simply of the penalty can never take away the imputability of the crime.[38] Such ignorance presupposes that the agent knows that he is violating the law. If the agent neglects to find out whether a penalty is attached to the violation of the law, the fault is his, and such ignorance does not take away imputability.[39]

Inadvertence is the actual state of mind in one who habitually knows the thing, but does not advert to it at the time.[40] The inadvertence may relate to the factual emergence of the act itself, or to the morality of the act. In either case the mind has the knowledge, but does not

[36] Swoboda, p. 151.

[37] Swoboda, p. 155: "In inculpable ignorance of law the physical act in itself may be entirely deliberate and voluntary, but the moral character of the act is not voluntary, because it is not known. In the case of ignorance of fact it is the full physical nature of the act, its essential qualities, or its effects that are not known and therefore involuntary." See also Michiels, I, 190.

[38] Canon 2202, § 2—"Ignorantia solius poenae imputabilitatem delicti non tollit, sed aliquantum minuit."

[39] Michiels, I, 192.

[40] Wernz-Vidal, VII, 98: "Inadvertentia est carentia actualis cognitionis, in eo qui habitualiter aliquid cognoscit: legem quis novit, sed dum operatur actu ad legem non advertit." See Swoboda, p. 123.

use it. It differs from ignorance in that ignorance implies that the knowledge was either never possessed, or if pospossessed was later totally lost.[41]

Ignorance must also be distinguished from error. Ignorance denotes the privation of knowledge, while error implies a false judgment. In error the mind judges, but its conclusion is contrary to the fact or to the law.[42]

Both inadvertence and error are to be judged by the same juridical principles that apply to ignorance.[43] Thus, if the inadvertence or the error is inculpable, and in no way the fault of the agent, the act will not be imputed to him. There is no imputability for the violation of laws that are unknown, or not adverted to, or about which error exists, if the ignorance, inadvertence, or error cannot be imputed to the agent.[44]

The burden of proving the existence of the ignorance, whether of the fact, or of the law, or simply of penalty, is incumbent upon him who asserts it. The canon law does not presume ignorance or error.[45] It is of the nature of law that it be known, otherwise the efficacy of the law would be destroyed.[46] It is for this reason that the law does not presume ignorance, but requires that it be proved by him who asserts it.

The imputability of a crime committed through ignorance is determined by the degree of culpability in the ignorance.[47] This is a purely subjective or moral basis,

[41] Swoboda, pp. 123-124.

[42] Swoboda, p. 120.

[43] Canon 2202, § 3—"Quae de ignorantia statuuntur, valent quoque de inadvertentia et errore."

[44] Coronata, IV, 41.

[45] Canon 16, § 2—"Ignorantia vel error circa legem aut poenam aut circa factum proprium aut circa factam alienum notorium generatim non praesumitur; . . . ." Cf. Vermeersch-Cresuen, I, 114.

[46] Beste, *Introductio in Codicem* (3. ed., Collegeville, Minn.: St. John's Abbey Press, 1946), p. 75 (hereafter cited as Beste): "Omnis lex natura sua obligationem cognitionis sui imponit, quia secus eius observantia redderetur impossibilis et ipsa legislatio inutilis."

[47] Canon 2202, § 1—". . . secus imputabilitas minuitur plus minusve pro ignorantiae ipsius culpabilitate." Cf. Swoboda, pp. 132 f.

and must be treated as such. In arriving at a satisfactory definition of culpable ignorance, one must take care to distinguish it from other uses of the word culpable. Culpable ignorance may be defined as a morally imputable lack of necessary and possible knowledge, in consequence of which the delinquent foresees that he is exposing himself to the proximate danger of violating a penal law. As Swoboda points out,[48] the four essential elements of culpable ignorance are: the knowledge must be necessary; the obligation must be not only physically but also morally possible of fulfillment; the delinquent must realize that he is ignorant; the obligation to know must have direct reference to the act about to be performed.

The role of measuring the degree of culpable ignorance in a criminal cause at court is that of the judge. It is not an easy task. He must consider the testimony and try to sift from it the precise degree of personal responsibility of the delinquent. Recourse must be had to the various degrees of guilt which are expounded by the moral theologians, since it is a question of subjective guilt. The canon law gives only the juridical principle that ignorance diminishes delictual imputability. Lacking any canonical directive, the judge must fall back upon degrees of culpability, such as crass, grave, affected, etc., which are discussed by moralists and are mentioned in canon 2229.[49]

The obligation to obey the law is not founded upon the threat of a penalty, but rather upon the authority of the legislator who has care of the common good. But whether or not a penalty is added in sanction of the law, does determine whether or not it is a penal law, though the obligation of obedience is not altered through the adding of a penal sanction. It is for this reason that canon 2202, § 2, states that ignorance simply of the penalty does not take away imputability, but can, in some measure, diminish it. The delinquent knew that the act was forbidden by

[48] Swoboda, pp. 132-135.

[49] Swoboda, pp. 157-162; Roberti, I, 105-110; Regatillo, II, 452; Michiels, I, 191; Wernz-Vidal, VII, 101.

law, and that he was bound in conscience to obey the law, and so the law will not excuse him from imputability, but will only consider it diminished.[50]

SECTION 5. UNCONTROLLABLE EVENTS

Events may occur which are violations of the law, but which the author thereof was not able to foresee, or even if he did foresee them, was not able to prevent. Such occurrences are called *casus fortuiti,* or uncontrollable events. One who gives rise to such an uncontrollable event is exempt from all imputability for the violation of the law.[51]

The law on uncontrollable events is a consistent application of the general principle or canonical jurisprudence that crimes are imputed to their author only when they are morally imputable to him. If the event could not be foreseen, it could not be willed, and hence is not morally imputable. If the events could be foreseen, but not prevented, the will of the agent is not its cause if he did not intend the crime, but intended only the act which he had a right to perform. In this latter case the author directly intends only the good action which he is free to do, and merely permits or suffers the violation of the law which he cannot prevent.[52]

There has often been proposed the question whether uncontrollable events should be imputed to an agent if he has engaged in some illicit activity. If one is hunting on forbidden territory, or outside of the hunting season, in violation of the law, and kills a man by purest mistake, should he not be held guilty of the crime by reason of his bad will in violating the law regarding hunting in that place, or in that season of the year? The common opinion is that there is no imputation of guilt for the uncontrollable

[50] Canon 2202, § 2—"Ignorantia solius poenae imputabilitatem delicti non tollit, sed aliquantum minuit." Cf. Swoboda, p. 164; Wernz-Vidal, VII, 104.

[51] Canon 2203, § 2—"Casus fortuitus qui praevideri vel cui praeviso occurri nequit, a qualibet imputabilitate eximit."

[52] Vermeersch-Creusen, III, 227; Regatillo, II, 454.

event. In the eyes of the moral law the agent is not guilty of the crime, and the eclesiastical law will not hold him for a criminal offense.[53]

SECTION 6. OMISSION OF DUE DILIGENCE

The omission of due diligence is one of the fonts or fundamentals or the imputability of crimes to a delinquent.[54] Two situations are envisioned in the phrase, omission of due diligence: the omission of the due diligence in not foreseeing that an act would violate the law, or, having foreseen the violation, in not having used the necessary precautions to avoid violating the law.[55] The law does not treat these in like manner as far as the imputability of such crimes is concerned.

If the delinquent neglects to use due diligence with the result that he does not foresee that he will violate the law, the imputability of the crime is diminished in the manner to be determined by the prudent judgment of the trial judge. The question of the foreseeability must be determined by the judge, and any diminution of imputability will follow from this determination.[56] The judge must attend to the gravity of the law, to the grave or light nature of the fault in not foreseeing, and to the condition or duty of the delinquent.[57]

In the instances in which the delinquent foresaw the violation of the law but failed to use the necessary precautions to avoid violating the law, the imputability of the crime is not diminished, but rather it is considered as proximate to malice.[58] A consideration of this situation

[53] Coronata, IV, 30.

[54] *Supra*, p. III-6.

[55] *Supra*, p. III-9.

[56] Canon 2203, § 1—"Si quis legem violaverit ex omissione debitae diligentiae, imputabilitas minuitur pro modo a prudenti iudice ex adiunctis determinando; . . ."

[57] Regatillo, II, 453-454.

[58] Canon 2203, §1—". . . quod si rem praeviderit, et nihilominus cautiones ad eam evitandam omiserit, quas diligens quivis adhibuisset, culpa est proxima dolo."

will demonstrate the necessity for this statement of the law. When the delinquent fails to foresee that he will violate the law, he is responsible for the crime because of his failure which was culpable; he has willed the violation of the law indirectly. No such indirect violation of the law is involved when the delinquent foresees the possible violation of the law, and yet fails to take adequate precautions to avoid the violation. His violation is wilful and direct. Such a violation is proximate to malice, and there is no diminution of the imputability of the crime.[59]

SECTION 7. FORCE

Force in canon law is defined as the use of such an external impetus that compels another to perform an action against his will.[60] The force under consideration has its origin in something outside of the agent. Physical force which takes away all liberty of action is considered here.[61]

In the introductory canons to the Second Book of the Code of Canon Law, the general principle in regard to force and its effect upon persons is stated in canon 103, § 1. All acts which a person, either moral or physical, performs by reason of extrinsic force which cannot be resisted are held to be null and void.[62] It makes no difference whethe the external force has been used for a morally good or evil reason.[63] If the employed force has deprived the agent of the use of his free will, the act is not a human act, but a mere act of a man. The agent is not so much acting as he is acted upon.[64]

Not only must the force be such that it deprives the

[59] Michiels, I, 193-194; Vermeersch-Creusen, III, 229.

[60] The dissertation on force and fear in relation to delictual imputability by McCoy treats of this subject at length. Cf. McCoy, p. 76; also Wernz-Vidal, VII, 108-109.

[61] Canon 2205, § 1—"Vis physica quae omnem adimit agendi facultatem, delictum prorsus excludit."

[62] Canon 103, § 1—"Actus, quod persona sive physica sive moralis ponit ex vi extrinseca, cui resisti, non possit, pro infectis habentur."

[63] Coronata, I, 176.

[64] McCoy, pp. 86-87.

agent of his free will, but the agent must also be positively unwilling to perform the act.[65] The act done becomes the act of the one who is applying the force, and not the deed of the agent in question. If the agent joins in the performance of the act with his own will when physical external force is present, then there is in reality a conspiracy for the performance of the act. Such an act would flow from the will of both him who causes the force and also of him who is forced.

The external force must be such that the agent is not actually able to resist. If the force could be resisted or impeded, then the conditions set in the canon are not verified. In the same manner there must be no imprudence or negligence on the part of the agent, for then he would be guilty in cause. While malice may be absent, there would be present the fact of criminal negligence from which imputability can arise.[66]

SECTION 8. LEGITIMATE DEFENSE AND PROVOCATION

In all cases of legitimate defense against an unjust aggressor, no crime is to be imputed to the agent as long as he uses due moderation in his defense.[67] The principle of law enunciated here is applicable not only to the defense of oneself against an unjust aggressor, but even to the defense of another whose rights are being unjustly attacked. The law does not distinguish between the defense of one's own rights, and those of another, but deals simply with legitimate defense.[68] Such defense of another's rights is foreseen especially in the cases involving husband and wife, blood relations or close friends.

For invoking the right of legitimate defense several

[65] Beste, p. 159: "Duo essentialiter ad vim requiruntur: 1. ut actus procedat a principio extrinseco; 2. ut ponatur cum repugnantia voluntatis."

[66] McCoy, p. 87; Coronata, IV, 35.

[67] Canon 2205, § 4—"Causa legitimae tutelae contra iniustum aggressorem, si debitum servetur moderamen, delictum omnino aufert; . . ."

[68] Coronata, IV, 36.

conditions are postulated in the law. The aggression must be one which is unjust. There cannot be a legitimate defense when the person who claims the right of self-defense is himself the cause or the instigator of the trouble. The foundation of this right of legitimate defense is that, in a conflict of rights between two or more parties, the rights of the innocent party are to be preferred. If the aggression is justifiable, there can be no right of legitimate defense against the agression.[69]

The second condition for the use of the right of legitimate defense is that due moderation must be observed. There must be a pressing necessity for the protecting of a right from an actual and imminently proximate danger of injury. If the injury has been inflicted in the past, or if there is some danger that it will be inflicted in the future, recourse should be had to the public authority which is responsible for repairing or preventing injury to the rights of the citizens. There must be lacking all other manner of avoiding the injury if one is to invoke the right of legitimate defense.[70]

There must be a proportion between the injury to be inflicted through the use of legitimate defense and the injury which would have been suffered by the one attacked. If the injury is reparable by other means, such as a suit for damages, there cannot be any infliction of injury to another's rights.[71]

Finally, the one who exercises the right of legitimate defense must not intend to inflict more injury upon the rights of the unjust aggressor, nor use more defense than is necessary to stop the aggression. If a mere striking will suffice to prevent the invasion or injury of one's rights, one may not mutilate the aggressor or take his life.[72]

[69] Regatillo, II, 458.

[70] Regatillo, II, 458; Vermeersch-Creusen, III, 228.

[71] Regatillo, II, 458.

[72] Coronata, IV, 36; Regatillo, II, 458; Vermeersch-Cresuen, III, 228.

The right of legitimate defense is not limited to the defense of life or limb, for it can also extend to the defense of valuable property which is of grave importance to its owner. Wernz-Vidal would permit the use of the right of legitimate defense to protect life, limb, liberty, chastity, and goods of great importance.[73]

If the delinquent has the right to use self-defense, but inflicts unnecessary injury upon the assailant, he is held liable for the unnecessary injury. The degree of imputability of the crime committed will be diminished in view of the use of legitimate defense,[74] but there is present at least negligence in not maintaining the proper proportion between the legitimate defense and the means which were actually necessary to attain this end.[75] It should be noted that other factors, such as passion, may also be present in the cases of legitimate defense, and these may be causes for diminishing or taking away altogether the imputability of the crime.

Provocation is the passion which is aroused by reason of some injury which is suffered.[76] The passion which is aroused may be wrath, such as arises because of injury to ourselves or to others, or sorrow, on account of the injury suffered by us or others. In the presence of such passions, there will be a disturbance of the mind which interferes with the full control of the intellect and the will.

The imputability of the crime will be diminished through the presence of a provocation which caused the crime.[77] The following conditions must first be verified if there is to exist a true provocation which will diminish imputability:

[73] Wernz-Vidal, VII, 119: "Quae autem de defensione vitae valent, pariter admittuntur de defensione membrorum, libertatis, pudicitiae, bonorum materialium magni momenti."

[74] Canon 2205, § 4—"... secus imputabilitatem tantummodo minuit, sicut etiam causa provocationis."

[75] Roberti, I, 157-158; Wernz-Vidal, VII, 120.

[76] Roberti, I, 159.

[77] Canon 2205, § 4—"... secus imputabilitatem tantummodo minuit, sicut etiam causa provocationis."

a. The one provoked must suffer from another's unjust action or his failure to act. It is not necessary that the unjust act be a crime in itself, but it must be an offense to the person, his rights, or to the person or rights of others closely bound to him by ties of blood or friendship. The provocation may be caused through word or deed.

b. There must actually be some disturbance of the mind as a result of the injury. The presence of unjust words or deeds which did not provoke another will have no effect upon imputability. The excitability of the individual must be considered by the judge along with the delinquent's sex, condition in life, etc.

The degree of the provocation will be judged from the gravity of the injury, the unjustness of the cause, and the time which elapsed between the provocation and the crime it caused. In many of these questions there is reciprocal provocation, and the judge must also take this into account.[78]

SECTION 9. PASSION

Man has both a spiritual and a sensual nature which impels him toward a good, or moves him to avoid an evil. It is the will which functions in the spiritual order; it is man's passions which function in the sensual order. The passions in man are movements of the sensual appetite which is either drawn to a sensual good, or repelled by a sensual evil.[79]

The concupiscible appetite in man draws him on to seek that which is good and agreeable to his sensual nature, or to avoid and flee that which is repugnant to his sensual nature.[80] These passions of the concupiscible appetite are

[78] Roberti, I, 160; Wernz-Vidal, VII, 121-122.

[79] Michiels, I, 220; Roberti, I, 160.

[80] St. Thomas, I, q. 81, a. 2: see Gilson *Christian Philosophy of St. Thomas Aquinas* (New York: Radom House, 1956), p. 239, (hereafter cited as Gilson).

six in number. The first three pertain to what is good: *love* is the movement toward a good considered in itself; *desire* is the movement of the senses toward a good which is not present; *joy* is the movement of the senses toward a good which is possessed. When the sensual object is an evil to be avoided, three corresponding concupiscible passions can come into play: *hatred* is the movement away from a thing considered evil in itself; *horror* is the movement of the senses away from an evil not present; *sorrow* is the movement of the senses in the presence of evil. All of these concupiscible passions consider the object under the aspect of good or evil alone.[81]

The five irascible passions consider the object not under the aspect of its agreeableness to man's sensual nature, but under the aspect of the difficult or the arduous.[82] The five irascible passions are: *hope,* which is the movement toward a good which one can attain; *desperation,* the movement toward a good which is fleeing; *audaciousness,* the movement against an evil which one attacks; *fear,* the movement by which one flees an evil; and *wrath,* the movement in the presence of an evil which one is suffering.[83]

If the passion precedes and prevents all deliberation of the intellect and consent of the will, imputability for the crime is taken away.[84] Both of these requirements are essential for the taking away of all imputability. The movement of the passion must precede the activity of the intellect and the will in such a manner that the agent is not guilty of any negligence. The passion must be of so grave a nature as to render it impossible for the intellect or the will to operate. This condition will seldom obtain, but should the exceptional circumstances be present, then nothing can be imputed to the agent. The actions are the

[81] Michiels, I, 220; Roberti, I, 161.

[82] Gilson, p. 239; see St. Thomas Aquinas, I, q. 81, a. 2.

[83] Michiels, I, 220; Roberti, I, 161.

[84] Canon 2206—"... et omnio tollit, si omnem mentis deliberationem et voluntatis consensum praededat et impediat."

acts of a man, but they are not human acts.[85] If the passions are aroused antecedently to the use of the intellect and the will, there results a disturbance of thought and a consequent limitation on the free exercise of the will. The greater the influence of the passions the less does man have control of his superior faculties.

Since ecclesiastical crimes must be morally imputable to their author, anything which interferes with the deliberation of the intellect or the freedom of the will affects the imputability of the crimes. Canon 2206 applies this principle of criminal law to the cases in which passion arises antecedently to the use of the intellect. Passion will diminish the imputability of the crime in a degree proportionate to the degree of the heat of the passion.[86] The more intense the passion, the less the degree of imputability.

The deliberate and voluntary arousing or nurturing of passion will increase the imputability of the crime.[87] The basis for increasing the imputability of a crime when the passions have been deliberately and voluntarily aroused or increased is the manifestation of malice which appears. There is a certain hardness of heart and a permeditation in arousing the passions for the purpose of perpetrating a crime. Such premeditation is a circumstance which increases the imputability of the crime.[88]

SECTION 10. FEAR, NECESSITY, AND HARDSHIP

If the evil which is to be avoided is of a spiritual instead of a sensual character, fear can arise in the spiritual appe-

[85] Michiels, I, 222; Roberti, I, 161; Vermeersch-Creusen, III, 228; Wernz-Vidal, VII, 123.

[86] Canon 2206—"... secus eam minuit plus minusve pro diverso passionis aestu; ..."

[87] Canon 2206—"Passio, si fuerit voluntarie et deliberate excitata vel nutrita, imputabilitatem potius auget; ..."

[88] Michiels, I, 221; Roberti, I, 180; Vermeersch-Creusen, III, 229; Wernz-Vidal, VII, 123.

tite, that is, in the will. Such fear will not hinder the free operation of the will, although the will is engaged in trying to avoid the evil.[89] The agent is left free to choose that which is the lesser of the evils presented—to violate the law, or to avoid the evil.

Necessity has been defined as "that objective condition of things, brought about in any manner whatsoever, in which an act that according to penal law is to be placed or omitted cannot be so placed or omitted because of an absolute or moral powerlessness, whether this latter be physical or spiritual."[90] The inability to obey the law is extrinsic to the agent, and is the result of causes such as nature, or the lack of the means necessary for life.

Grave hardship involves a relative powerlessness for the fulfillment of the law. One can indeed fulfill the law, but only at the price of a hardship which the legislator does not intend that one should suffer for the sake of a compliance with his law.

When the penal law involved is a purely ecclesiastical law, the legislator is not considered to impose the observance of his law in the face of even relatively grave fear, necessity or hardship. Imputability is taken away.[91] The existence of these situations which conflict with the law creates such a serious hardship that the legislator is considered not to have intended to include the case in his law. Moralists commonly hold to this same principle in the case of an affirmative divine law, positive or natural.[92]

The use of the word *plerumque*, "as a rule," in canon 2205, § 2, makes room for a legislator to command the observance of a penal law which is purely an ecclesiastical law, although it is difficult and arduous, or in spite of any grave fear or similar factor. Thus, in a given exceptional

[89] McCoy, p. 77.

[90] McCoy, p. 83. Cf. Michiels, I, 199; Wernz-Vidal, VII, 113.

[91] Canon 2205, 2: "Metus quoque gravis, etiam relative tantum, necessitas, imo et grave incommodum, plerumque delictum, si agatur de legibus mere ecclesiasticis, penitus tollunt."

[92] McCoy, p. 89.

and expressed situation, fear, necessity, or hardship would not excuse from observing the law.

If the law is not a purely ecclesiastical law, but is a restatement of the divine law, either natural or positive, the observance of the law is required no matter what the fear, necessity or hardship. That which God has commanded for the spiritual good of the Church is to be preferred to the private good of an individual. A serious transgression would always be imputed to its author as a crime.[93] There are three categories of such divine commands.

Some actions are intrinsically evil, and cannot possibly be made objectively good actions. Into this category will fall acts which violate the fundamental precepts of the natural law, such as blasphemy, perjury, abortion, murder, theft, etc. Other acts, such as apostasy, heresy and schism, are also intrinsically evil.[94]

The commission of certain other crimes involves contempt of the faith or of ecclesiastical authority by the very nature of the act. It is this objective contempt which determines whether or not the act falls into this second category, and not the subjective contempt of the delinquent. Included in this category are: casting away of the Sacred Species, usurpation of priestly functions, superstition, attempted marriage before a non-Catholic minister, heresy, conspiracy against the authority of the Roman Pontiff or against a bishop, etc.[95]

Finally, some crimes will draw people away from the faith or from a sound moral life, and result in their eternal damnation. These crimes endanger another's salvation either because of the scandal involved, or by the very nature of the act. No man can be excused of a crime because of fear, necessity or hardship if the salvation of

[93] McCoy, p. 90: "And the reason for this is that some spiritual good, either of God or of the Church, or of individual souls is involved. Such a good is essentially superior to the private, natural good of the agent and therefore must be obtained at all costs."

[94] McCoy, p. 91.

[95] McCoy, pp. 92-96.

another's soul is the price. Among such delicts should be included: the administration of the sacraments to those who are forbidden to receive them, the absolution of one's accomplice, the consecration of a bishop without a papal mandate, simony in regard to the sacraments, the discarding of the clerical garb and the violation of the obligation of celibacy when scandal would be involved.[96]

If a crime is intrinsically evil, eventuates in contempt of the faith or of ecclesiastical authority, or causes damage to souls, then grave fear, necessity or hardship will not take away imputability for the crime, but it will diminish the gravity of the crime.[97] The crimes committed in these circumstances are willed, seriously sinful, and will be punished by the law, although diminution of the penalty is recognized.

SECTION 11. DIGNITY OF THE PERSON OFFENDED, OR OF THE DELINQUENT, AND ABUSE OF AUTHORITY OR OFFICE

Real circumstances are those which surround the object of the criminal act, i.e., the thing or the person. Included in these real circumstances are the fact of being a minor, the place where the act was perpetrated (in church, in public), the time (during Lent, or during Mass), the amount of damage inflicted, and the manner of acting. Other circumstances are personal, such as the special malice or cruelty of the delinquent, the dignity of the delinquent, premeditation, the dignity of the one offended, and abuse of authority or office.[98]

Not all of these circumstances are given in the law, but they are implied in the wording of canon 2207. This canon enumerates only three specific circumstances which will increase the imputability of the crime, but this enumera-

[96] McCoy, pp. 97-98.

[97] Canon 2205, § 3—"Si vero actus sit intrinsece malus aut vergat in contemptum fidei vel eccesiasticae auctoritatis vel in animarum damnum, causae, de quibus in § 2, delicti imputabilitatem minuunt quidem, sed non auferunt."

[98] Wernz-Vidal, VII, 124-125.

tion is obviously not an all-inclusion list. The canon states that besides other aggravating circumstances, the greater dignity of the person who commits the crime, or of the one who is offended by the crime, or also the abuse of authority or office are factors of similar import which can serve to intensify the crime.[99]

The greater the dignity of the delinquent the greater the scandal which is given to the community, and the greater is the effect of the bad example upon the community. For this reason the fact that the delinquent is a bishop rather than a simple priest, or that the delinquent is the governor of a State rather than a common citizen, would increase the imputability of the crime.

Upon those who possess a certain added dignity in the community there rests an added burden not to violate the law, and thus to endanger the salvation of others by their bad example. Since the canon does not distinguish between ecclesiastical or civil dignity, both are to be included as circumstances which aggravate the crime.[100]

On the other hand, while the personal damage inflicted upon one who is constituted in some dignity is not increased by reason of his dignity, there does result an added injury to the position or the dignity which he possesses. An attack upon the person of a police officer is offensive not only to the officer, but also to the authority which he represents. In like manner an attack upon a bishop is an offense to the ecclesiastical society, just as an attack upon one's father would strike at the foundation of the most primary of all societies, the family.

Sometimes the law modifies the nature of the crime in accord with the dignity of the one offended.[101] Canon 2343

[99] Canon 2207—"Praeter alia adiuncta aggravantia, delictum augetur: 1° Pro maiore dignitate personae quae delictum committit, aut quae delicto offenditur; 2° Ex abusu auctoritatis vel officii ad delictum patrandum."

[100] Canon 2207. Cf. Vermeersch-Creusen, III, 229; Wernz-Vidal, VII, 125; Roberti, I, 165-168; Michiels, I, 224-226.

[101] Canon 2207.

applies this principle with the various penalties there enacted for those who lay violent hands upon the various ecclesiastical dignitaries enumerated. This same principle is applicable with reference to civil dignities also.[102]

The abuse of authority or of an office increases the imputability of the crime.[103] Authority and office are granted to an individual for the furthering of the common good of the society. The abuse of this office or authority causes grave scandal to the community and tends to weaken the structure of the society. It is for this reason that the abuse of the authority or office in the commission of a crime is an aggravating cause which increases the imputability of the crime. It makes no difference if the authority or office is ecclesiastical of civil.[104]

Particular crimes of the abuse of authority are punished as special crimes in Title XIX of the Fifth Book of the Code of Canon Law. Since the abuse of the authority or the office is an essential element of these crimes, this fact does not increase their imputability.

SECTION 12. RECIDIVISM

In order to avoid confusion with the theological concept of a recidivist, and to fix precisely the canonical definition, canon 2208 defines a recidivist in the legal sense as one who, after a condemnatory sentence, again commits a crime of the same genus and in such circumstances in regard to the thing and especially the time that it can be judged prudently that the delinquent is pertinacious in his bad will.[105]

[102] Michiels, I, 227-228; Roberti, I, 168-171; Wernz-Vidal, VII, 125.

[103] Canon 2207.

[104] Wernz-Vidal, VII, 126; Vermeersch-Creusen, III, 229-230; Roberti, I, 171-174; Michiels, I, 231.

[105] Canon 2208, § 1—"Recidivus sensu iuris est qui post condemnationem rursus committit delictum eiusdem generis et in talibus rerum ac praesertim temporis adiunctis ut eiusdem pertinacia in mala voluntate prudenter coniici possit."

From an examination of this definition one sees that the following conditions must be verified before the delinquent can be regarded as a recidivist:

a. The delinquent must again commit a new crime which is perfectly distinct from that which he committed in the past. The continuation of an old crime (such as concubinage), or the completion of a crime that was initiated in the past will not make a delinquent a recidivist.

b. The new crime must be of the same genus as the crime which was committed in the past. The same type of crime will not suffice, it must be generically identical with the earlier committed crime. After a theft, a subsequent act of theft would suffice, but not embezzlement.

c. The delinquent must have been condemned for the prior crime. The prior offense must have been adjudicated as a crime, and must have become a settled issue (*res iudicata*), according to the norms of canons 1902 and 1903.

d. The judge must be able to declare that the new crime arose from the pertinacious bad will which was in existence in the old crime. The circumstances of the case, but especially that of time, are important factors for the one who is called on to make this determination. If a great period of time has elapsed between the crimes, and the delinquent has shown signs of contrition for his earlier crime and some signs of reform, the second crime will not make him a recidivist.[106]

The recidivist, and anyone who has committed previous crimes even of a different genus, are to be held more profoundly responsible for the subsequent crime, and accord-

[106] For an excellent treatment of the definition of the recidivist see Michiels, I, 232-236. Cf. also Roberti, I, 174-179; and Wernz-Vidal, VII, 126-134.

ingly the penalty is to be increased.[107] The term recidivist should be reserved for those who fit the definition found in the Code, and the use of the terms *general recidivist* and *specifiic recidivist,* as used by some authors,[108] should be avoided.

Article II. In American Criminal Law

The common law and the American criminal law hold responsible for their criminal acts all persons who possess the requisite mental capacity and who have acted freely.[109] Any exceptions to this rule must be clearly and explicitly expressed in the law. Blackstone was willing to except only those for whom the law had made an exception, and did not make room for any exceptions which might arise but which the law had not considered. His words leave no room for doubt:

> ... for the general rule is, that no person shall be excused from punishment for disobedience to the laws of his country, excepting such as are expressly defined and exempted by the laws themselves.[110]

Whether one possesses criminal capacity may be a question of fact to be rebutted, as in the case of those alleged to be insane, or it may be a question of presumption of law, as in the case of infants. The law sometimes justifies, or excuses from, a violation by reason of circumstances, such as legitimate defense. In any of these cases the exemption must be clearly stated in the law.

Civil law systems are more inclined to change the very

[107] Canon 2208, § 2—"Qui pluries deliquerit etiam diverso in genere, suam auget culpabilitatem."

[108] E.G., by Vermeersch-Creusen, III, 230; Coronata, IV, rr; Brys, *Juris Canonici Compendium* (2 vols., Brugis: Desclie (Braumert et Sii, 1947-1949), II, 417.

[109] "As a general rule, any person possessing the mental capacity required by law, who voluntarily commits any criminal act, is responsible for such act and is subject to punishment for it."— Burdick, I, 196.

[110] Blackstone, IV, 17.

nature of the crime than simply to acknowledge causes as mitigating the inmputability of the crime. The various degrees of unlawful homicide: premeditated, second degree, manslaughter, and involuntary manslaughter, are established in lieu of expressing any elaborate system for diminishing imputability for the unlawful killing of another. Thus less consideration is given to the causes which increase or diminish imputability for crimes.

SECTION 1. AGE

Children do not possess the same mental capacity and control of their will as adults are presumed to possess. It is for this reason that the law has long considered it proper to maintain a distinction between the criminal capacity of children and that of adults. Blackstone indicated that this is based upon their defect of the understanding.[111] The emphasis in our modern jurisprudence is rather the protection of the child from penal punishments. Thus Burdick writes:

> Children of tender years must be protected from penal consequences for their irresponsible acts, and the public must be protected from the responsible and even malicious acts of young offenders.[112]

The common law borrowed from the Roman Law its norm regarding the incapacity of infants to commit crimes. The child under the age of seven was immune from all punishment for his criminal acts.[113] This presumption of law remains unchanged in most of the Anglo-American systems. England has raised the age to eight, Texas has increased it to nine, and Illinois and Georgia have raised the age of infancy to ten years of age. Only Arkansas has raised the age as high as twelve years.[114]

[111] "First we will consider the case of infance, or nonage, which is a defect of the understanding."—Blackstone, IV, 20.

[112] Burdick, I, 202; see also May, p. 36.

[113] "During the first stage of infancy . . . they (children) were not punishable for any crime."—Blackstone, IV, 20.

[114] Burdick, I, 205.

The presumption of lack of capacity in an infant is one which cannot be rebutted. The law will not inquire into the mental capacity of an infant to determine if he really did possess discretion and accordingly should be held responsible for his criminal act. Thus Chief Justice Faircloth wrote:

> An infant under seven years of age cannot be indicted and punished for any offense because of the irrebuttable presumption that he is *doli incapax.*[115]

Between the ages of seven and fourteen a child is held not to have criminal capacity, but this is a presumption which can be rebutted.[116] If the offender is between the ages of seven and fourteen, the question of his criminal capacity becomes one of fact to be proved in the face of the presumption in his favor. Thus is the case of the State *vs.* Yeargam, the defendant was found guilty of "shooting craps" in spite of the fact that he was under fourteen years of age. The defendant was held to be abe to discern between good and evil; and so it was held he could have been punished. The court explained the principle of law very clearly:

> Between seven and fourteen years of age, an infant is presumed to be innocent and incapable of committing crime, but that presumption, in certain cases, may be rebutted, if it appears to the court and jury that he is capable of discerning between good and evil, and in such cases he may be punished.[117]

The closer in age the child approaches to the age of full criminal capacity, the more likely will be the conclusion that he could discern between good and evil. In the case of the State *vs.* George, Ezekiel R. George, under fourteen years of age, was found guilty of arson. Chief Justice Love

[115] State *vs.* Yeargam, 117 N.C. 706, 23 S.E. 153 (1895).

[116] Blackstone informs us that the common law changed the age from twelve, fixed under the Saxon law, to fourteen. See Blackstone, IV, 22.

[117] State *vs.* Yeargam, 117 N.C. 706, 23 S.E. 153 (1895).

in his opinion quoted from 3 Greenleaf on Evidence #4 in justifying the conviction:

> The second is the period from seven to fourteen. During this period the presumption continues, but is no longer conclusive, and grows gradually weaker as the age advances toward fourteen.[118]

The States of New York and Oklahoma have raised the age of full criminal capacity from fourteen to sixteen years, but the majority of the courts still follow the common law rule since these have been no statutory changes.

The rise of Juvenile Courts has not affected these principles of law, but rather has changed the methods of handling youthful offenders. The majority of these statutes place the criminal acts of those under sixteen years of age under the jurisdiction of Juvenile Courts, which will apply remedial penalties, as well as punishments for the offenses. The Federal Juvenile Delinquency Act places the age at seventeen years,[119] while others have raised the age to eighteen.[120] The legality of depriving the Courts of Oyer and Terminer of their jurisdiction has been upheld.[121] Some statutes require the Juvenile Court to have the case removed to the regular criminal courts in cases of murder, rape, or robbery.

SECTION 2. INSANITY

Those who are insane are excused from guilt for criminal offenses which they may commit. This was the rule at common law according to Blackstone,[122] and is the law today.[123] The law holds that such persons labor under such a defect of understanding and lack of freedom of the will, that they cannot be held responsible for their crimes.

The defense of insanity is a complete defense but it must

[118] State *vs.* George, 20 Del. 57, 54 Atl. 745 (1902).

[119] U.S.C.A. Tit. 18, secs. 921-929.

[120] Burdick, I, 204-206; Snyder, pp. 310-311.

[121] State *vs.* Goldberg, 124 N.J.L. 272, Atl. 2d 299 (1940).

[122] "In criminal cases, therefore, idiots and lunatics are not chargeable for their own acts, if committed when under these incapacities: no, not even for treason itself."—Blackstone, IV, 24.

be proved in favor of the defendant for whom it is asserted. For the defendant there must be proof that he is insane under the law, and not necessarily according to the standards of medical evidence. It is insanity in contemplation of law, not of psychiatry which counts. Thus Burdick writes:

> The main question when one is accused of crime, and insanity is alleged in defense, is, did the accused, when the act was committed, have, in contemplation of law (not of psychological theory), the mental capacity required to make him legally responsible.[124]

The principles of insanity as a defense were formulated in McNaughton's Case in 1843, and these rules have been the basis for almost all subsequent legislation. England, Canada, and all of the American States except New Hampshire, Rhode Island, and more recently New Jersey and the District of Columbia, follow the McNaughton Rule. The principles are set forth most clearly in the *New York Penal Law*:

> A person is not excused from criminal liability as an idiot, imbecile, lunatic, or insane person, except upon proof that, at the time of committing the alleged criminal act, he was laboring under such a defect of reason as:
> 1. Not to know the nature and quality of the act he was doing;
> 2. Not to know the act was wrong.[125]

The number of cases which fall under the first number of this section are not great. The inability to know the nature and quality of the act is limited to those actions which are done almost without consciousness. The common example is the action of an epileptic while in seizure, and about which he is not even aware. Criminal acts done in such a state are rare, but if they occur, there is no crim-

[123] Burdick, I, 275-279; Snyder, pp. 312-313; May, p. 48.

[124] Burdick, I, 268.

[125] *New York Penal Law,* Sec. 1120.

inal capacity, and the defendant is not responsible for them.[126]

The majority of cases will come under the second number, which treats of those who are so mentally ill that they do not know the act is wrong. The law does not usually detail what exactly is meant by the words "idiot, imbecile, lunatic, or insane person," but permits the court to hear the testimony of medical experts on the subject. The determination of whether the defendant was laboring under any of these conditions is one of fact to be made by the jury. In view of the differences of opinion among medical experts, there seems to be no more certain method of procedure.[127]

The question of what is meant by the word "wrong" has come in for more precise determination by the courts. It is now settled that by "wrong" is meant "moral" wrong, and not "legal" wrong. There is not need to know that the "wrong" has also been forbidden by the law. The inability to know that it is "wrong" must flow from the mental disease, and not from any mere absence of knowledge. In the case of the People *vs.* Schmidt all of these points were made clear:

> By morally wrong is meant morally wrong by by those standards deemed to prevail throughout our jurisdiction.... Moreover, it is not enough that the actor does not know the act is wrong because he happens not to notice; the want of knowledge of wrongfulness must be the result of want of mental capacity to distinguish between right and wrong with regard to the act being done.[128]

The principles set forth above, as based on McNaughton's Case, are the only test for insanity in Canada, England and in twenty-five of the American States.

The doctrine of irresistible impulse is admitted in twenty-

[126] People *vs.* Burgess, 153 N.Y. 561, 47 N.E. 889 (1897).

[127] Burdick, I, 279; Snyder, p. 313.

[128] People *vs.* Schmidt, 216 N.Y. 324, 110 N.E. 945 (1915); see also Snyder, p. 383, and Burdick, I, 280-281.

one American jurisdictions: Alabama, Arkansas, Colorado, Connecticut, Delaware, Georgia, Illinois, Indiana, Kentucky, Louisiana, Massachusetts, Michigan, Montana, New Mexico, Ohio, Pennsylvania, Utah, Vermont, Virginia, Washington, and Wyoming.[129] The doctrine of irresistible impulse does not consider the inability of the defendant to know right fro mwrong; he possesses this faculty. The defendant is not held liable for his criminal act because he was not able to control his will, and thus not able to avoid breaking the law. His thought processes were in working condition, but the delinquent was not able to abide by what his intellect knew to be right.[130]

The inability to control the will must be the direct result of a mental disturbance. The disease must be the cause of the crime, and not a mere interference from the passions.[131] The irresistible impulse should not be confused with loss of control of the will due to provocation, anger, passion, or hatred. Many of the jurisdictions refuse to admit irresistible impulse because they fear it will break down the law and permit many to go free. In the opinion of not a few, the doctrine of irresistible impulse is covered by the principles of the McNaughton Rule.[132]

An insane delusion is a false belief caused by a diseased mind; it is an imagined state of affairs. The insane delusion falls under the McNaughton Rule and protects the defendant from punishment for the criminal act.[133] A mere mistake of judgment is not an insane delusion since it is not founded upon a diseased mind.[134] When the insane delusion is asserted as a defense in a criminal trial, the

[129] Burdick, I, 277.

[130] Burdick, I, 284-285; Snyder, pp. 314-315; May, p. 49.

[131] Korsak *vs.* State, 202 Ark. 921, 154 S.W. 2d. 348 (1941); People *vs.* Barbari, 149 N.Y. 256, 43 N.E. 635 (1896).

[132] State *vs.* Simenson, 195 Minn. 258, 262 N.W. 638 (1935); People *vs.* Voresca, 353 Ill. 52 186 N.E. 607, (1933); Comm. *vs.* Schroeder, 302 Pa. 1, 152 Atl. 835 (1930).

[133] Snyder, pp. 313-314; Burdick, I, 282; May, p. 52.

[134] Draus, *vs.* State, 108 Neb. 331, 187 N.W. 895 (1922); State *vs.* Jones, 50 N.H. 369 (1871).

imagined state of affairs must be such as would have excused from the crime if it had been true. Snyder summed up this point in these words:

> Insane delusion is recognized as sustaining the defense of insanity if the imagined state of affairs, were it to exist in fact, would be a defense.[135]

Some few jurisdictions have begun to accept the plea of temporary insanity as a defense to criminal prosecution.[136] The defendant is held to be sane before and after the criminal act, but temporarily insane at the time he committed it. It has been admitted in cases where in one finds his spouse in the act of adultery, and in cases of like great passion.[137] The same plea was refused in the case wherein the spouse subsequently killed the paramour.[138] The majority of the jurisdictions have criticized the doctrine of temporary insanity, and called it an application of the "unwritten law." It is, however, gaining strength in more and more States. Michigan allows the plea, but places the defendant in a State mental hospital until he can be discharged as safe to live again in society.

SECTION. 3 DRUNKENNESS, DRUGS, SLEEP

Voluntary drunkenness not only was no defense to criminal prosecution at common law, but, according to Blackstone, it aggravated the crime.[139] This is still the law in the Anglo-American jurisdiction if one omits the aggrava-

[135] Snyder, p. 313; see Rozien *vs.* State, 185 Ga. 317 (1938); Hubbard *vs.* State, 197 Ga. 77, 28 S.E. 2d. 115 (1943).

[136] Burdick, I, 286.

[137] Fannon *vs.* Comm. 295 Ky. 817, 175 S.W. 2d 531 (1943); Dulty *vs.* State, 131 Wis. 178, 111 N.W. 222 (1907).

[138] Wilkes *vs.* State, 215 Ala. 428, 110 S.W. 911 (1927).

[139] "As to artificial, voluntarily contracted madness, by drunkenness or intoxication, which depriving men of their reason, puts them in a temporary frenzy; our law looks upon this as an aggravation of the offense, rather than as an excuse for any criminal misbehaviour."—Blackstone, IV, 25.

tion, which is seldom considered today. Burdick sums up the attitude of the law in these words:

> The fact that one commits a crime while drunk, as a result of his own voluntary act, does not affect his responsibility, for, as a general rule, drunkenness is no defense to crime.[140]

There is some confusion and conflict in the United States concerning the effect of drunkenness upon those crimes which demand a specific intent. If the crime is defined in such a manner that a specific intent is required as essential to the crime, then this intent must be actually present. Thus, crimes such as larceny and assault with the intent to kill, are not proved by mere evidence of their commission, but the specific intention must also be proved. If the defendant was drunk, even if voluntarily so, was it possible for him to have the specific intent required by the law?

Larceny requires the intent to deprive the owner of his property. In the case of Edwards *vs.* State, Edwards stole a cab while voluntarily drunk, and defended himself on the ground that he did not remember the theft, and so did not intend to deprive the owner of his cab. The trial judge refused to accept the plea and instructed the jury that "voluntary drunkenness is no defense to crime." The appellate court reversed the trial judge and ordered a new trial. This court held that the presence of specific intent was necessary to constitute the crime, and that the determination of its presence or absence by reason of drunkenness was a question of fact which should have been submitted to the jury. Chief Justice Smith wrote in his opinion:

> Drunkenness is at least quasi-criminal, and if a person while voluntarily drunk commits a criminal act, the drunkenness supplies the criminal intent, except where a specific intent is necessary to constitute the crime charged.[141]

The same principle has been applied to assault with the

[140] Burdick, I, 213-214; see Snyder, p. 320; May, pp. 55-56.

[141] Edwards *vs.* State, 178 Miss. 696, 174 So. 57 (1937).

intent to kill.[142] The defendant may be convicted of simple assault, since the drunkenness will supply the criminal intent, but assault with the intent to kill can be defended by a plea of drunkenness which would make the intent impossible.[143]

That a criminal act was committed while one was involuntarily drunk will be a defense to criminal prosecution. The defendant can in no way be held to have willed the drunkenness or the resultant crime.[144] This is the principle in all jurisdictions, and it makes no difference how the drunkenness came about, as long as it was not voluntary. Snyder states the principle of law in these words:

> Where, however, one becomes intoxicated, without his consent, by means of force or fraud of another, whatever form of intoxicant may be employed, this condition is that of involuntary drunkenness; and a criminal act committed by him while in such a state of mind is entitled to whatever defense the circumstances justify.[145]

The use of narcotics or other drugs will be governed by the same principles of law as is drunkenness. If the defendant was voluntarily under the influence of drugs, he is held responsible for his criminal actions. If the use of the narcotics was involuntary, he is not held accountable.[146] This principle is upheld in all jurisdictions.[147]

SECTION 4. IGNORANCE AND MISTAKE

Although there is a difference between ignorance and mistake, there is little difference in the law applicable to both. Ignorance is the lack of knowledge; the person just does not know. In mistake, on the other hand, the person

[142] State *vs. Cather*, 121 Iowa 106, 96 N.W. 722 (1903).

[143] Snyder, p. 321; May, pp. 56-59.

[144] Choate *vs.* State, 190 Okla., C.R. 169, 197 Pac. 1060 (1921).

[145] Snyder, p. 322; May, p. 60.

[146] People *vs.* Lun Dum Dong, 26 Cal. Apl. (2d.) 135, 78 Pac. (2d.) 1026, (1938).

[147] Burdick, I, 220; Synder, p. 322.

presumes that he knows, but in fact he does not.[148] Burdick brings out the distinction by comparing them:

> Ignorance is passive and does not pretend to knowledge; mistake presumes to know when it does not.[149]

Ignorance of the law, or a mistake of law, is a defect of the intellect which affects the freedom of the agent. If he does not know, his will is unable to command. In spite of this the common law held that ignorance of the law is no excuse. Blackstone indicated that there exists a presumption that all men know the law, and hence ignorance or mistake of law cannot be asserted as a defense:

> For a mistake in point of law, which every person of discretion not only may but is bound and presumed to know, is in criminal cases no sort of defense. *Ignorantia iuris, quod quisque tenetur scire, neminem excusat,* is as well the maxim of our own law as it was of the Roman.[150]

The modern-day rule on ignorance or mistake of law follows that of the common law. The administration of justice would take on an impossible burden if men were permitted to assert their lack of knowledge as a defense. Ignorant men would be paid a premium for their ignorance, while wise men would suffer for having known the law. These reasons keep the civil law from considering ignorance of the law as a defense.[151]

Ignorance of law can be a defense in some few cases which have a nature peculiar to themselves. The crime of perjury, e.g., demands that the delinquent lie under oath. Hence, one who is ignorant or mistaken cannot be guilty of perjury since he is not lying.[152] In other cases

148 Langston *vs.* Langston, 147 Ga. 318, 93 S.E. 892 (1905).

149 Burdick, I, 234; see May, pp. 60-64.

150 Blackstone, IV, 27.

151 Armour Packing Co. *vs.* U.S., 209 U.S. 56, 52 L. Ed. 681, 28 S.C. 428 (1908); Weston *vs.* Comm., Ill. Pa. St. 251, 2 Atl. 191 (1886); State *vs.* Foster, 22 R.I. 163, 46 Atl. 833 (1900).

152 Freeman *vs.* Croon, 172 N.C. 524 90 S.E. 523 (1916); see Snyder, p. 286.

the absence of intent to violate the law because of ignorance or mistake is supplied by the intention to do the act. In State *vs.* Yeargam, the court said:

> Among persons of full age ignorance of the law is no excuse, nor is the absence of any intent to violate it available as a defense, but it is the intent to do an act which is a violation of law that makes an actor guilty.[153]

A mistake of fact or ignorance of a fact will be a defense to a criminal action. A man's will does not even want to place the criminal act. There can be no crime until the criminal intent and the criminal act meet. The simplest examples bring out the point most clearly. One who is ignorant or mistaken about the fact that the money he is spending is counterfeit is not guilty of a crime.[154] If one contracts marriage believing his previous spouse is dead, he does not commit the crime of bigamy.[155] The taking and carrying away of articles mistakenly thought to be one's own is not larceny.[156] The general principle is summed up by Burdick in these words:

> A sincere and reasonable mistake of fact, which had it been true would have made the act lawful, usually constitutes a complete defense to a charge of crime.[157]

The ignorance or mistake must be not only reasonable but also honest and sincere. If no reasonable man would have been so mistaken, the defense will fall. In like manner the ignorance should not be a result of the negligence of the defendant. These principles are exemplified in State *vs.* Lintner:

> If one shuts his eyes to facts, he should not be permitted to plead his ignorance of them.[158]

[153] State *vs.* Yergam, 117 N.C. 706, 23 S.E. 154 (1895).

[154] Pigman *vs.* State, 14 Ohio 555 (1846).

[155] Reg. *vs.* Tolson, 23 Q. B. D. 168 (1889).

[156] Dean *vs.* State, 41 Fla. 291, 26 S. 638 (1899).

[157] Burdick, I, 238; see Snyder, p. 282.

[158] State *vs.* Lintner, 141 Kan. 505 41 Pac. 2d. 103G (1936); see also Snyder, p. 290.

The civil authority has the power to pass laws which bind all even though there is a mistake of fact. The exercise of the police power in protecting the public safety, health, morals and general welfare is sufficient reason to justify the passing of such laws. Actions which violate such aspects of the common welfare are prohibited no matter what one's intention or state of mind.[159]

A very brief, but accurate, summary of the law of mistake or ignorance of law or fact is contained in People *vs.* Cohen:

> Everyone is presumed to know the law—both common and statutory. An honest mistake of fact will generally shield one from a criminal prosecution, but one's mistake of the law furnishes no exemption from criminal responsibility.[160]

SECTION 5. ACCIDENT OR MISADVENTURE

Both the common law and modern-day American jurisprudence will excuse a defendant from criminal liability if the criminal act occurred through accident or misadventure. Blackstone stated that misadventure is the commission of a criminal act without any intention of doing wrong, which act is performed while one is engaged in doing a good and licit act.[161] Absence of fault or malice is of the essence of misadventure.[162]

The courts have held that accident or misadventure can be considered in the cases of hunting and other sports.[163] Similarly, if the proper care and reasonable knowledge of his science is had and used, a medical doctor cannot be held responsible for accidents that may occur.[164]

159 Burdick, I, 240.

160 People *vs.* Cohen, 358 Ill. 326, 331, 193 N.E. 150 (1934).

161 Blackstone, IV, 182.

162 Burdick, II, 143; see also State *vs.* Watson, 26 Del. 273, 82 Atl. 1086 (1912).

163 Comm. *vs.* Lewis, Addison (Pa.) 270 (1796); State *vs.* Hardie, 47 Iowa 647 (1878); U.S. *vs.* Lipsett, 156 Fed. 65 (1907).

164 Comm. *vs.* Thompson, 6 Mass. 134 (1809).

SECTION 6. COERCION, COMPULSION, AND NECESSITY

The common law admitted coercion, compulsion and necessity as a defense to a criminal prosecution. These were considered as taking away the free will, and thus as excusing acts done under stress of unavoidable force and compulsion. Blackstone stated the effect of coercion and necessity in these words:

> A sixth species of defect of will is that arising from compulsion and inevitable necessity. These are a constraint upon the will whereby a man is urged to do that which his judgment disapproves; and which, it is to be presumed, his will (if left to itself) would reject. As punishments are therefore only inflicted for the abuse of that free will which God has given to man, it is highly just and equitable that a man should be excused for those acts which are done through unavoidable force and compulsion.[165]

The terms coercion, compulsion and necessity are not used with any precise distinction between them in the present-day law. Coercion has the connotation of threats, intimidation, or indirect means to put pressure upon a person, while compulsion has the meaning of force and physical restraint or constraint. Necessity is used to express unavoidable circumstances, conditions, or factors which leave the actor with no choice but to violate the law. In many jurisdictions these terms are interchanged freely.[166]

The presence of coercion is a fact to be determined by the jury, and failure to permit the jury to take it into consideration is reversible error. Thus in Nall *vs.* Comm. the defendant was threatened by a woman with a gun who ordered him to break and enter. The trial judge refused to let the jury consider the fact of coercion as a defense, and the appellate court ordered a new trial.[167]

At common law there was a rebuttable presumption

[165] Blackstone, IV, 27.

[166] See May, p. 38; Burdick, I, 261.

[167] Nall *vs.* Comm., 208 Ky. 700 (1925); 271 S.W. 1059.

that a woman in the presence of her husband was under his coercion if she committed a crime. This presumption has been abrogated in the Federal law of the United States and in many of the State jurisdictions.[168]

The precise nature of necessity has never been clearly established in the law. The inability to choose any except one of two evils constituted a necessity according to Blackstone.[169] Anything which would constitute violence to society or to the safety thereof has been termed necessity.[170] Both at common law and in modern jurisprudence hunger is not such a necessity that it will excuse from the crime of theft.[171] According to Snyder, such considerations may be used for a mitigation of the penalty to be inflicted.[172]

The principles of law governing coercion, compulsion, and necessity are well summed up in the following statement from Burdick's treatise:

> Since every crime requires a willing or voluntary mind, it may be a defense to a criminal charge that the criminal act was not committed voluntarily but was the result of coercion, compulsion, or necessity.[173]

SECTION 7. LEGITIMATE DEFENSE AND PROVOCATION

The defense pleaded to a criminal action that the dedefendant did it in legitimate defense of himself or of another is usually treated in a discussing of the law regarding homicide, but the same principles may apply to the commission of any crime. Legitimate defense is concerned

168 Snyder, p. 310.

169 Blackstone, IV, 30.

170 Snyder, p. 292; Burdick, I, 262; Moor *vs.* State, 23 Ala. App. 432 127 Sam. 796 (1930); State *vs.* Patterson, 117 Ore. 153, 241 Pac. 977 (1925).

171 Blackstone, IV, 31; State *vs.* Moe, 174 Wash. 303, 22 Pac. 2d. 985 (1933); see also Burdick, II, 321.

172 Snyder, p. 291.

173 Burdick, I, 260; see Harris *vs.* State, 91 Tex. Cr. R. 446, 241 S.W. 175 (1922); People *vs.* Jackenson, 247 N.Y. 36, 159 N.E. 715 (1925).

only with excusable homicide, and not with one that is justifiable.

A justifiable homicide is one in which there is no guilt at all. The defendant in this case acts in virtue of his office, e.g., an executioner, or for the advancement of public justice, e.g., a police officer attempting to arrest a felon. Not only is the defenant acting without fault, but he is doing a positively good act in the furtherance of his duty.[174]

Excusable homicide, or excusable defense, involves the application of the principle that one has the right to defend oneself or another from an unjust aggression. Burdick expressed the doctrine thus:

> ...a homicide where one without being in any fault at the time is attacked by another in such a way or manner that he has reasonable ground to believe that he is in immediate danger of death or great bodily injury, and necessarily, as he reasonably believes, slays his assailant in order to protect himself.[175]

The aggression must be real, or reasonably thought to be real, if it is not actually present.[176] The threat of slight or inconsequential damage will not excuse from the commission of a homicide. There must be danger of great bodily harm which is present, and which can be avoided by no other means.[177] The necessity of retreat prior to an exercise of the right of legitimate defense was part of the common law, and is required today. The one attacked must retreat as far as possible, and then not use any more force than is necessary to avoid the danger to himself.[178]

[174] Blackstone, IV, 178-182; Burdick, I, 126.

[175] Burdick, II, 126; Ex parte Warren 31 Tex. 143 (1868); State *vs.* Blackburn 23 Del. 479, 75 Atl. 536 (1892).

[176] May, pp. 69-73; Rowe *vs.* U.S. 164 U.S. 546, 41 L. Ed. 547, 17 S.C. 172 (1896); Padgett *vs.* State, 40 Fla. 451, 24 S. 145, (1898); People *vs.* Grimes 132 Col. 30; see also Snyder, pp. 303-304.

[177] Acers *vs.* U.S. 164 U.S. 388 48 L. Ed. 481, 17 S.C. 91 (1896); Owens *vs.* U.S., 130 Fed. 279 (1904); see Burdick, II, 130.

[178] Blackstone, IV, 184-186; Bingham *vs.* State, 203 Ala. 163, 82 S. 192 (1919; Brown *vs.* U.S. 256 U.S. 355, 65 L. Ed. 961, 41 S.C. 501 (1921); see Snyder, p. 304; May, p. 71.

The right of legitimate defense is not limited to defending oneself alone, but extends to defending any man. The *New York Penal Law* includes husband, wife, parent, child, brother, sister, master, servant, or any other person in his presence or company, as persons who may be defended.[179] The one who takes up the defense of another puts himself into the same position as the one he is defending. If the one defended has no right to defend himself, or only a limited right, then the defender has no right or only a limited right.[180] If the one defended turns out to be a fleeing felon, and thus without the right of defense, the defender cannot plead the legitimate defense of another.

The defense of property is a legitimate defense to a criminal prosecution, if the defender did not use more force than was necessary. It is a question of serious doubt if life may be taken to defend property, although some courts seem to hold this as possible if the property is of great value.[181]

Since the first use of the expression, "a man's home is his castle" in Cemoyne's Case[182] in 1604, the law has explicitly protected a man's right to guard his home with all the force necessary, even the taking of life. It has been stated that no man need retreat further than his home, and also that the home is more precious to man than his own life. Whatever the reason, however, the law extends him an excuse, even for homicide, if he is defending the fireside and hearth.[183]

Provocation is the act by which one person brings upon

[179] New York Penal Law, sec. 1055; see California Penal Code, sec. 197, 198.

[180] Burdick, II, 134; Snyder, p. 303; May, p. 73; see Kansas General Statutes, Ch. 21 at 404.

[181] May, p. 75; Storey *vs.* State, 71 Ala. 329 (1882); State *vs.* Dooley, 121 Mo. 591, 26 S.W. 558 (1894).

[182] Semoyne's Case, 5 Coke 91, 77 Eng. Rep. 194 (1604).

[183] State *vs.* Bradley, 126 S.C. 528, 120 S.E. 240 (1923); State *vs.* Preece, 116 W. Va. 176, 179 S.E. 524 (1935); State *vs.* Martin, 30 Wis. 216 (1872); see May, p. 77.

himself the attack of another by angering his assailant.[184] The courts have held that words alone will not constitute a provocation in law, but will act to mitigate the penalty to be inflicted.[185] The commission of even slightly suggestive action with the wife of another has been held to be sufficient provocation to justify the use of the force necessary to stop it.[186]

SECTION 8. RECIDIVISM

The legislature has the power to provide heavier penalties for habitual criminal.[187] When the legislature exercises this power there is no new offense established, nor is there an additional punishment for the prior offense, but the offender is punished more severely because he manifests a depravity which merits greater punishment.[188]

The problem of whether to punish the recidivist with greater penalties has been a vexing one since early colonial days. Until the beginning of the twentieth century, the problem was always that of punishing the special recidivist, a criminal who falls back into the same crime. The passing of the Volstead Act, and the rising popularity of the Crime Commission in the 1920's focused the problem upon the question of punishment of the criminal who manifested his maliciousness by any kind of a subsequent crime. The statute books began to fill with laws to punish the general recidivist. Today, 41 States and the District of Columbia have general recidivist laws.[189]

[184] Snyder, p. 298.

[185] State *vs.* Miller, 231 Iowa 863, 2 N.W. 2d. 290 (1892); see Snyder, p. 299.

[186] Redding *vs.* State, 25 Ga. App. 233, 102 S.E. 845 (1920).

[187] Ex Parte Kuwitzky, 135 Neb. 466, 282 N.W. 395 (1939); Comm. *vs.* Smith, 324 Pa. 73, 109 Atl. 786 (1920).

[188] Sullivan *vs.* Ash, 302 U.S. 51, 82 L. Ed. 43, 58 S.C. 59 (1937); People *vs.* Rose, 26 Cal. App. 2d. 513, 79 Pac. 779, (1938); Emert *vs.* Thorn, 292 N.Y.S. 58, (1932).

[189] The Federal Government and the States of Arkansas, Delaware, Maryland, Mississippi, North Carolina, South Carolina, and Tennessee do not. See the excellent account in: Brown, "The Treat-

The precise definition of a recidivist varies considerably. In fifteen States and the District of Columbia, any person sentenced to a penitentiary term, having previously served one or more such penitentiary terms, is a recidivist. Fourteen States define a recidivist as one who has been convicted of a felony, and who has already been convicted of one or more previous felonies. Thirteen States list the number of crimes which constitute the prior and present crimes necessary for one to be considered a recidivist. Finally, four States define a recidivist as one who commits a misdemeanor following prior conviction for a misdemeanor.[190]

Not all States punish as a recidivist the second offender. Twenty-eight States and the District of Columbia double the punishment for the second offense, and impose life in prison only if the first offense could have been life. A third offense is required in twenty-five States to label one a recidivist, and of these only six make the life penalty mandatory.[191] The rest double or triple the punishment. Eighteen States require a fourth offense to invoke recidivist penalties, with thirteen requiring life penalties, and all of them making life penalties possible.[192]

The courts have been reluctant to use the recidivist penalties, and have shied away from enforcing the statutes. This they have often done by stretching the interpretation of the recidivist statutes. Thus in People ex rel. Marclay *vs.* Lawes, Warden et al, the court held that a plea of guilty to three prior felonies which merited two suspended sentences did not imply three convictions or prior felonies that would come under the recidivist statute.[193] It has been set-

ment of the Recidivist in the United States" *The Canadian Bar Review,* (Ottawa: National Printers Limited 1922—) XXIII (1945), 640. (Hereafter cited as Brown).

190 Brown, p. 645.

191 Colorado, Indiana, Kentucky, Texas, Washington, West Virginia. See Brown, p. 647.

192 Brown, p. 647.

193 People ex rel. Marclay *vs.* Lawes, Warden et al, 254 N.Y. 249, 172 N.E. 487, (1930).

tled in all jurisdictions that the prior crimes must have come to final judgment, and not merely by pending before the courts.[194]

Article III. Comparison of Causes Affecting Imputability

The Anglo-American law is more inclined to change the naturė of the crime, and thus to multiply the number of crimes, than to give general rules for increasing or diminishing the imputability of crimes for specific causes. Thus there is less in the civil law on this subject.

Infants beneath the age of seven are held absolutely incapable of criminal intent in both systems of law. The ecclesiastical law considers imputability diminished in those under twenty-one years of age, the more so the more they approach the age of infancy. The civil law holds all persons over the age of fourteen, or sixteen in some jurisdictions, capable of criminal intent, but protects those between this age and the age of infancy by a rebuttable presumption of incapacity for crime. The civil law has special Juvenile Courts for those under sixteen or eighteen years of age, while the ecclesiastical law does not, though it does provide for educative penalties.

The habitually insane are held incapable of crime in both systems of law. The civil law generally follows the rule that the defendant is guilty if he has the ability to distinguish between right and wrong, as set forth in McNaughton's Case. The ecclesiastical courts rely more heavily upon the testimony of the medical experts regarding the mental capacity of the accused. Both systems leave the final determination to the jury or the judge. The doctrine of insane delusions is considered separately by the civil law, while the ecclesiastical law includes it under the law governing the insane.

Temporary insanity and irresistitble impulse are ad-

[194] Neal *vs.* Comm. 221 Ky. 239, 298 S.W. 704 (1927); see also 24 C. J. S. #1958-1973.

mitted as defenses by some of the civil jurisdictions, and are open to consideration in the ecclesiastical courts under the heading of "passions" in mitigation of imputability.

Voluntary drunkenness is not a defense in either system of law, but rather increases the responsibility in the early common law and in the ecclesiastical law. Involuntary drunkenness is a defense in both systems of law. The use of drugs, hypnosis, and sleep are treated as is drunkenness in both laws.

Ignorance or mistake of fact will be an absolute defense in both systems, but ignorance or mistake of law is admitted as a defense only in the ecclesiastical law. Ignorance simply of the penalty will diminish the imputability in ecclesiastical law only.

Accident or misadventure, or what is called an uncontrollable event, is an absolute defense in both systems of law.

Absolutely irresistible force, compulsion, coercion or necessity is a defense in civil law, and in the ecclesiastical law, too, as long as the crime is of a purely ecclesiastical character. Something less than grave force, compulsion, coercion, or necessity will diminish the imputability in ecclesiastical law.

Legitimate defense of onself or another is admitted by both systems of jurisprudence, as longs as: it is defense against an unjust aggressor, there is no other way of avoiding the injury, and no more force than necessary is used. Using too much force in legitimate defense mitigates the imputability in ecclesiastical law, and subjects one to punishment for a lesser crime in civil law. Provocation can excuse in civil law, but will only diminish the responsibility in ecclesiastical law.

The law on recidivists is similar in both systems, but the ecclesiastical law does not set down precise penalties for recidivists. The civil law does not make one a recidivist until a second, a third, or a fourth offense. The ecclesiastical law defines a recidivist in terms of a second defense.

CONCLUSIONS

1. The ecclesiastical criminal law considers itself as only one part of the moral order, and hence subject to the guiding principles of morality. American criminal law considers itself an independent science. Cf. pp. 24-25, 35-37.

2. The Church requires as an essential part of the definition of a crime that the criminal act be morally imputable to its author. Unless the delinquent is guilty before God and his own conscience, no criminal act can be imputed to him. The American criminal law requires only that the author of the act intend and do it; the guilty mind, *mens rea,* is required in only a minority of cases, most of which are of common law origin. Cf. pp. 13-14, 19-23.

3. Malice or criminal negligence must be present before any person can be held responsible for a criminal act in either system of law. Causing an external violation of the law raises a rebuttable presumption that malice is present. Cf. pp. 27-32, 37-45.

4. Anything which destroys the freedom of the will takes away responsibility for the crime in both the ecclesiastical and the American criminal law systems. Thus if insanity, infancy, involuntary drunkenness, ignorance of fact, uncontrollable events, force, hardship, and necessity, take away the freedom of the will, they will also take away imputability. Fear and legitimate defense are also admitted as absolute defenses. Cf. pp. 47-71, 76-93.

5. Ecclesiastical criminal law recognizes ignorance of the law as a defense to criminal prosecution, but it must be pleaded and proved in order to overthrow the presumption that ignorance of the law is not present. The American criminal law holds that ignorance of the law excuses no one, which has given rise to absolute liability statutes. Cf. pp. 54-59, 87-90.

6. Temporary insanity is admitted as a defense in only

a few of the American jurisdictions. Ecclesiastical law permits the defense of passion either as a complete defense or in mitigation of the imputability of the crime. Cf. pp. 66-69, 84-85.

7. The recidivist is punished more severely than the first offender in both systems of law. Cf. pp. 71-76, 90-93.

8. The ecclesiastical law increases the imputability of the crime with the increased dignity of the defender, or of the one offended, or with the abuse of authority or office. American jurisdictions prefer to establish new crimes according to the circumstances rather than to increase the imputability. Cf. pp. 69-71.

It is not surprising to find that the American criminal law and the ecclesiastical criminal law have so many comcomn juridical principles, since both were considered together in the Middle Ages, when the civil law and the ecclesiastical law were guided by the general principles of the moral order. They share a common Christian tradition and heritage. The philosophical differences between these two systems in the present state of the law are to be attributed to the rejection to a great extent by the civil law of the principle of moral imputability as the basis for criminal imputability.

BIBLIOGRAPHY

SOURCES

CANON LAW:

Codex Iuris Canonicii Pii X Pontificiis Maximi iussu digestus, Benedicti Papae XV auctoritate promulgatus, Praefatione, Fontium Annotatione et Indice Analytico-Alphabetico ab Emo Petro Card. Gasparri Auctus, Romae, Typis Polyglottis Vaticanis, 1917; reimpressio, 1934.

AMERICAN CIVIL LAW:

"Articles of Confederation," Newton, Arthur P., *Federal and Unified Constitutions*, London: Longmans, Green & Co., 1923.

West's California Digest, St. Paul, Minn.: West Publishing Co., 1951.

United States Code Annotated, St. Paul, Minn.: West Publishing Co., 1951.

Kansas Digest, St. Paul, Minn.: West Publishing Co., 1951.

The Consolidated Laws of New York Annotated, St. Paul, Minn.: West Publishing Co., 1955.

Purdon's Pennsylvania Statutes Annotated, St. Paul, Minn.: West Publishing Co., 1950.

ROMAN LAW:

Corpus Iuris Civilis, Vol. I, *Institutiones*—recognovit P. Krueger; *Digesta*—recognovit T. Mommsen, retractavit P. Krueger; Vol. II, *Codex Iustinionus*—recognovit et retractavit P. Krueger; Vol. III, *Novellae Constitutiones*—recognovit R. Schoell, opus Schoellii morte interceptum absolvit G. Kroll, Berolini, 1928-1929.

REFERENCE WORKS

CANON LAW:

Abbo, John A.-Hannan, Jerome D., *The Sacred Canons*, 2 vols., St. Louis: B. Herder Book Co., 1952.

Aquinas, Thomas, *Summa Theologia*, Vol. I, 1950; Vol. II, 1948; Vol. III, 1948, Taurini, Roma: Marietti.

———, *In Libros Politicorum Aristotelis Expositio*, Taurini, Roma: Marietti, 1951.

Bender, Ludovicus, *Ius Publicum Ecclesiasticum*, Bussum in Hollandia: Paulus Brand, 1948.

———, *Philosophia Iuris*, 2. ed., Romae: Officium Libri Catholici, 1955.

Beste, Udalricus, *Introductio in Codicem*, 3 ed., Collegeville, Minn.: St. John's Abbey Press, 1946.

Wernz, Franciscus X.-Vidal, Petrus, *Ius Canonicum ad Normam Co-*
Blat, Albertus, *Commentarium Textus Codicis Iuris Canonici*, 6 vols., Romae, 1919-1927.

Brooke, Z. N., *The English Church and the Papacy from the Conquest to the Reign of John*, Cambridge: The University Press, 1931.

Brys, J., *Juris Canonici Compendium*, 2 vols., Brugis: Desclie de Brouwert et Sii, 1947-1949.

Cappello, Felix M., *Summa Iuris Canonici*, 3. ed., 3 vols., Romae: Apud Aedes Universitatis Gregorianae, 1938-1948.

Cocchi, Guidus, *Commentarium in Codicem Iuris Canonici*, 8 vols., Vol. VIII, *De Delictis et Poenis*, 4. ed., Taurinorum Augustae: Marietti, 1938.

Coronata, Matthaeus Conte a, *Institutiones Iuris Canonici*, 5 vols., Vol. I, 4. ed., 1949; Vol. II, 4. ed., 1951; Vol. III, 3. ed., 1948; Vol. IV, 3. ed., 1948; Vol. V, 3. ed., 1951; Taurini-Romae: Marietti.

Doronzo, Emmanuel, *De Poenitentia*, 4 vols., Vol. II, *De Contritione et Confessione*, Milwaukee: Bruce, 1951.

Gilson, Etienne, *Christian Philosophy of St. Thomas Aquinas*, New York: Random House, 1956.

McCoy, Alan E., *Force and Fear in Relation to Delictual Imputability and Penal Responsibility*, The Catholic University of America Canon Law Studies, n. 200, Washington, D.C.: The Catholic University of America Press, 1944.

Michiels, Gommarus, *De Delictis et Poenis*, Vol. I, Lublin: Universitas Catholica, 1934.

Moorman, John R. H., *Church Life in England in the Thirteenth Century*, Cambridge: At the University Press, 1955.

Ottaviani, Alaphridus, *Institutiones Iuris Publici Ecclesiastici*, 2 vols., Romae: Typis Polyglottis Vaticanis, Vol. I, 3. ed., 1947; Vol. II, 2. ed., 1936.

Pantin, W. A., *The English Church in the Fourteenth Century*, Cambridge: At the University Press, 1955.

Roberti, Franciscus, *De Delictis et Poenis*, Vol. I, Partes I et II, Romae: Apud Custodiam Librariam Pontificii Instituti Utriusque Iuris, 1930-1938.

Regatillo, Eduardus F., *Institutiones Iuris Canonici*, 4 ed., 2 vols., Santander: Sal Terrae, 1951.

Swoboda, Innocent R., *Ignorance in Relation to the Imputability of Delicts*, The Catholic University of America Canon Law
Studies, n. 143, Washington, D.C.: The Catholic University of America Press, 1941.

Vermeersch, Arthurus-Creusen, Josephus, *Epitome Iuris Canonici*, 6. ed., 3 vols., Mechliniae-Romae: H. Dessain, 1937- 1946.

dicis Exactum, 7 vols. in 8, Romae: Apud Aedes Universitatis Gregorianae, Vol. I, 2. ed., 1952; Vol. II, 3. ed., 1943; Vol. III, 1933; Vol. IV, Pars I, 1934; Vol. IV, Pars II, 1935; Vol. V, 3. ed., 1946; Vol. VI, 2. ed., 1949; Vol. VII, 2. ed. 1951.

Woywod, Stanislaus, *A Practical Commentary on the Code of Canon Law*, revised by Callistus Smith, revised and enlarged edition, 2 vols., New York: Joseph F. Wagner, Inc., 1948.

AMERICAN CIVIL LAW:

American Jurisprudence, 58 Vols. and Indices, Rochester, N.Y.: Bancroft Whitney Co., 1935-1952.

Blackstone, Wm., *Commentaries on the Laws of England with a Commentary by Chief Justice Sharswood*, 4 vols. in 2, Philadelphia: Lippincott, 1898.

Bouvier, John, *Law Dictionary and Concise Encyclopedia*, 2 vols., Vol. I, 8 ed., St. Paul, Minn.: West Publishing Co., 1914.

Burdick, William L., *The Law of Crimes*, 3 vols., Albany: Matthew Bender & Co., 1946.

Corpus Juris Secundum, 95 Vols. and Indices, Brooklyn, N.Y.: The American Law Book Co., 1936-1951.

Del Vecchio, Georgio, *Philosophy of Law*, Washington, D.C.: The Catholic University of America Press, 1953.

Grotius, Hugo, *De Jure Belli ac Pacis Libri Tres*, 2 vols., Oxford: At the Clarendon Press, 1925.

Hobbes, Thomas, *Leviathan*, New York: The Macmillan Co., 1947.

Holmes, Oliver W., Jr., *The Common Law*, Boston: Little, Brown & Co., 1881.

Hughes, Philip, *The Reformation in England*, 3 vols., London: Hollis & Carter, 1950-1954.

Locke, John, *Essays on the Law of Nature*, Oxford: At the Clarendon Press, 1954.

May, John W., *Law of Crimes*, 4. ed., Boston: Little, Brown & Co., 1938.

McKay, George, *The Law of Community Property*, 2. ed., Indianapolis: The Bobbs-Merrill Co., 1925.

Morris, Richard B., *Studies in the History of American Law*, New York: Columbia University Press, 1930.

Pollock, Frederick-Maitland, Frederick W., *History of English Law*, 2. vols., 2. ed., Cambridge: At the University Press, 1909.

Report of the Ecclesiastical Courts Commission, Vol. I, London, 1883.

Rommen, Heinrich, *The Natural Law*, St. Louis, Mo.: B. Herder Book Co., 1949.

Rousseau, Jean Jacques, *Du Contrat Social*, Paris: Aubier, 1943.

Snyder, Orville, *Criminal Justice*, New York: Prentice-Hall, Inc., 1953.

ARTICLES

Brown, George K., "The Treatment of the Recidivist in the United States," *The Canadian Bar Review*, XXIII, 1945, 630-683.

Mueller, Gerhard O. W., "Crime, Tort and the Primitive," *The Journal of Criminal Law, Criminology and Police Science*, XLVI, 1955, 303-332.

———, "*Mens Rea*," *West Virginia Law Review*, LVIII, 1955, 34-68.

Sayre, Francis B., "The Present Significance of *Mens Rea*," *Harvard Legal Essays*, Cambridge, Mass.: Harvard University Press, 1934, pp. 399-417.

PERIODICALS

The Canadian Bar Review, Ottawa: National Printers Limited, 1922—

The Journal of Criminal Law, Criminology and Police Science, Evanston, Ill.: The Northwestern University Press, 1910—

West Virginia Law Review, Morgantown, W. Va.: The University of West Virginia Press, 1894—

CASES CITED

Acers *vs.* U.S., 164 U.S. 388; 48 L. Ed. 481; 17 S.C. 91 (1896).

Allbriton *vs.* Winona, 181 Miss. 75; 175 S. 799 (1938).

American Banana Co. *vs.* United Fruit Co., 213 U.S. 347; 55 L. Ed. 826; 29 S.C. 511 (1909).

Armour Packing Co. *vs.* U.S., 209 U.S. 56; 52 L. Ed. 681; 28 S.C. 428 (1908).

Bingham *vs.* State, 203 Ala. 162; 82 S. 192 (1919).

Blackmer *vs.* U.S., 284 US. 421; 76 L. Ed. 375; 52 S.C. 252 (1932).

Branch *vs.* State, 41 Tex. 622 (1874).

Brown *vs.* State, 23 Del. 159; 74 Atl. 836 (1909).

Brown *vs.* U.S., 256 U.S. 335; 65 L. Ed. 961; 41 S.C. 501 (1921).

Chandler *vs.* State, 141 Ind. 106; 39 N.E. 444 (1894).

Chisholm *vs.* Georgia, 2 Dall. U.S. 415; 1 L. Ed. 418 (1793).

Choate *vs.* State, 190 Okla. C. R. 169; 197 Pac. 1060 (1921).

Comm. *vs.* Hawkins, 157 Mass. 551; 32 N.E. 862 (1893).

Comm. *vs.* Lewis, Addison (Pa.) 279 (1796).

Comm. *vs.* Schroeder, 302 Pa. 1; 152 Atl. 835 (1930).

Comm. *vs.* Smith, 266 Pa. 511; 109 Atl. 786 (1920).

Comm. *vs.* Smith, 324 Pa. 73; 187 Atl. 387 (1936).

Comm. *vs.* Thompson, 6 Mass. 134 (1809).

Comm. *vs.* Weiss, 139 Pa. 247; 21 Atl. 10 (1891).

Comm. *vs.* Wheeler, 205 Mass. 384; 91 N.W. 415 (1910).

Dean *vs.* State, 41 Fla. 291; 26 S. 638 (1899).

Dulty *vs.* State, 131 Wis. 178; 111 N.W. 222 (1907).

Duncan *vs.* State, 7 Humph. (Tenn.) 148 (1846).

Edwards *vs.* State, 178 Miss. 696; 174 S. 57 (1937).
Emert *vs.* Thorn, 292 N.Y.S. 58; 54 N.E. 2d. 155 (1936).
Ex parte Kuwitzky, 135 Neb. 466; 282 N.W. 396 (1938).
Ex parte Smith, 135 Mo. 223; 36 S.W. 628 (1896).
Ex parte Warren, 31 Tex. 143 (1868).
Fannon *vs.* Comm., 295 Ky. 817; 175 S.W. ed. 531 (1943).
Freeman *vs.* Croon, 172 N.C. 524; 90 S.E. 523 (1916).
Green *vs.* State, 41 Ala. 419 (1868).
Green *vs.* State, 150 Ga. 121; 102 S.E. 813 (1920).
Harris *vs.* State, 91 Tex. Cr. R. 446; 241 S.W. 175 (1922).
Hubbard *vs.* State, 197 Ga. 77; 28 S.E. ed. 115 (1943).
Korsak *vs.* State, 202 Ark. 921; 154 S.W. 2d. 348 (1941).
Fraus *vs.* State, 108 Neb. 331; 187 N.W. 895 (1922).
Lambert *vs.* People, 76 N.Y. 220 (1879).
Langston *vs.* Langtons, 147 Ga. 318; 93 S.E. 892 (1917).
Lansing *vs.* State, 73 Neb. 124; 102 N.W. 254 (1905).
McDonald *vs.* People, 47 Ill. 533 (1868).
Moor *vs.* State, 23 Ala. App. 432; 127 S. 796 (1930).
Nall *vs.* Comm., 208 Ky. 700; 271 S.W. 1059 (1925).
Neal *vs.* Comm., 221 Ky. 239; 298 S.W. 704 (1927).
Owens *vs.* U.S., 130 Fed. 279 (1904).
Padgett *vs.* State, 40 Fla. 451; 24 S. 145 (1898).
People *vs.* Barbari, 149 N.Y. 256; 43 N.E. 635 (1896).
People *vs.* Burgess, 153 N.Y. 561; 47 N.E. 889 (1897).
People *vs.* Cohen, 358 Ill. 331; 193 N.E. 150 (1934).
People *vs.* Grimes, 132 Cal. 30; 64 Pac. 101 (1901).
People *vs.* Jackenson, 247 N.Y. 36; 159 N.E. 715 (1928).
People *vs.* Lun Dum Dong, 26 Cal. App. 2d. 135; 78 Pac. 2d. 1026 (1938).
People *vs.* Rockwell, 39 Mich. 503 (1878).
People *vs.* Rose, 26 Cal. App. 2d. 513; 79 Pac. 739 (1938).
People *vs.* Schmidt, 216 N.Y. 324; 110 N.E. 845 (1915).
People *vs.* Vorecha, 353 Ill. 52; 186 N.E. 607 (1933).
People ex rel. Marcloy *vs.* Lawes, Warden et al., 254 N.Y. 249; 172 N.E. 487 (1930).
Peay *vs.* Comm., 181 Ky. 396; 205 S.W. 404 (1918).
Pigman *vs.* State, 14 Ohio 555 (1846).
Pool *vs.* State, 87 Ga. 526; 13 S.E. 556 (1891).
Redding *vs.* State, 25 Ga. App. 233; 102 S.E. 845 (1920).
Reg. *vs.* Tolson, 23 Q.B.D. 168 (1889).
Respublica *vs.* Malin, I Dall. (U.S.) 33; 1 L. Ed. 25 (1778).
Rowe *vs.* U.S., 164 U.S. 546; 41 L. Ed. 547; 17 S.C. 172 (1896).
Rozier *vs.* State, 185 Ga. 317; 195 S.E. 172 (1938).
Rutledge Co-operative Association *vs.* Baughman, 153 Md. 297; 138 Atl. 29 (1927).

Semoyne's Case, 5 Coke 91; 77 Eng. Rep. 194 (1604).
State *vs.* Blackburn, 23 Del. 479; 75 Atl. 536 (1892).
State *vs.* Bradley, 126 S.C. 528; 120 S.E. 240 (1923).
State *vs.* Cather, 121 Iowa 106; 96 N.W. 722 (1903).
State *vs.* Dooley, 121 Mo. 591; 26 S.W. 558 (1894).
State *vs.* Field, 131 N.M. 120; 241 Pac. 1027 (1936).
State *vs.* Foster, 22 R.I. 163; 46 Atl. 811 (1900).
State *vs.* George, 20 Del. 57; 54 Atl. 745 (1902).
State *vs.* Goldberg, 124 N.J.L. 272; 11 Atl. 2d. 299 (1940).
State *vs.* Hardie, 47 Iowa 647 (1878).
State *vs.* Inman, 239 Ala. 348; 195 S. 448 (1940).
State *vs.* Jones, 50 N.H. 369 (1871).
State *vs.* Lintner, 141 Kan. 505; 41 Pac. 2d. 1036 (1936).
State *vs.* Martin, 30 Wis. 216 (1872).
State *vs.* McBrayer, 98 N.C. 619; 2 S.E. 755 (1887).
State *vs.* Miller, 9 Houst. (Del). 564; 32 Atl. 137 (1892).
State *vs.* Miller, 231 Iowa 863; 2 N.W. 2d. 290 (1942).
State *vs.* Mills, 6 Penn. (Del.) 497; 69 Atl. 841 (1908).
State *vs.* Moe, 174 Wash. 303; 22 Pac. 2d. 985 (1933).
State *vs.* Moore, 129 Iowa 514; 106 N.W. 16 (1906).
State *vs.* Morgan, 98 N.C. 641; 3 S.E. 927 (1887).
State *vs.* O'Brien, 32 N.J.L. 169 (1867).
State *vs.* Patterson, 117 Ore. 153; 241 Pac. 977 (1925).
State *vs.* Preece, 116 W. Va. 176; 179 S.E. 524 (1935).
State *vs.* Rider, 90 Mo. 54; 1 S.W. 825 (1886).
State *vs.* Roselli, 109 Kan. 33; 198 Pac. 195 (1921).
State *vs.* Schull, 66 S. Dak. 102; 279 N.W. 241 (1931).
State *vs.* Simenson, 195 Minn. 258; 262 N.W. 638 (1935).
State *vs.* Watson, 26 Del. 273; 82 Atl. 1086 (1912).
State *vs.* Yeargan, 117 N.C. 706; 23 S.E. 154 (1895).
Stein *vs.* State, 37 Ala. 125 (1861).
Storey *vs.* State, 71 Ala. 329 (1882).
Stringfellow *vs.* State, 26 Miss. 157 (1853).
Sullivan *vs.* Ash, 302 U.S. 51; 82 L. Ed. 43; 58 S.C. 59 (1937).
Theide *vs.* Town of Scandia Valley, 217 Minn. 218; 14 N.W. ed. 400 (1944).
U.S. *vs.* Balint, 258 U.S. 250; 66 L. Ed. 604; 42 S.C. 301 (1922).
U.S. *vs.* Bradford, 148 Fed. 413 (1905).
U.S. *vs.* Dennis, 341 U.S. 494; 95 L. Ed. 1137; 71 S.C. 857 (1951).
U.S. *vs.* Eaton, 144 U.S. 677; 36 L. Ed. 591; 12 S.C. 764 (1892).
U.S. *vs.* Frick, 259 Fed. 673 (1919).
U.S. *vs.* Harmon, 45 Fed. 414 (1891).
U.S. *vs.* Lipsett, 156 Fed. 65 (1907).
Weston *vs.* Comm., 111 Pa. 251; 2 Atl. 191 (1886).
Wilkes *vs.* State, 215 Ala. 428; 110 S. 911 (1927).

BIOGRAPHICAL NOTE

Rev. John Joseph McGrath was born in Pittsburgh, Pennsylvania, on December 12, 1922. He attended the parochial grade schools in Pittsburgh and Mount Lebanon Public High School. In 1943 he was awarded a Bachelor of Arts Degree from Duquesne University. He attended Duquesne University School of Law and received his Bachelor of Laws Degree in 1947. He entered Mount St. Mary's Seminary of the West, Cincinnati, Ohio, and was ordained to the priesthood on May 29, 1954, by the Most Rev. John King Mussio, Bishop of Steubenville, as a priest of that diocese. He entered Catholic University of America in the fall of 1954 and was awarded the Bachelor of Canon Law Degree in June of 1955, and the Licentiate of Canon Law Degree in June of 1956.

ALPHABETICAL INDEX

www.ingramcontent.com/pod-product-compliance
Lightning Source LLC
LaVergne TN
LVHW050200080826
844660LV00012B/322

* 9 7 8 0 8 1 3 2 2 5 4 5 6 *